ALFRED HITCHCOCK'S BOOK OF HORROR STORIES No. 5

Drawn from the best of *Alfred Hitchcock's Mystery Magazine*, this is a collection of chilling stories from the masters of horror: John Lutz, Rufus King, Avram Davidson – and many others.

Also by the same author,
and available in Coronet Books:

Alfred Hitchcock's Book of Horror Stories No. 5

Alfred Hitchcock
Edited by Eleanor Sullivan

CORONET BOOKS
Hodder and Stoughton

Copyright © Davis Publications, Inc. 1978

First published in Great Britain in 1983 by Max Reinhardt
Ltd, as the second half of a hardback edition entitled
TALES TO MAKE YOUR BLOOD RUN COLD

Coronet edition 1986

British Library C.I.P.

Alfred Hitchcock's book of horror stories: no. 5.
  1. Horror tales, English
  I. Hitchcock, Alfred   II. Sullivan, Eleanor
  823'.01'0816[FS]   PR1309.H6

ISBN 0-340-38506-5

Printed and bound in Great Britain for
Hodder and Stoughton Paperbacks, a
division of Hodder and Stoughton Ltd.,
Mill Road, Dunton Green, Sevenoaks,
Kent (Editorial Office: 47 Bedford
Square, London, WC1 3DP) by
Hunt Barnard Ltd., Aylesbury, Bucks.

ACKNOWLEDGEMENTS

'CAREER MAN' by James Holding; © by H.S.D. Publications, Inc.; reprinted by permission of Scott Meredith Literary Agency, Inc.

'A FLOWER IN HER HAIR' by Pauline C. Smith; copyright H.S.D. Publications, Inc., 1967; reprinted by permission of the author.

'PROXY' by Talmage Powell; © 1966 by H.S.D. Publications, Inc.; reprinted by permission of Scott Meredith Literary Agency, Inc.

'THE INTANGIBLE THREAT' by Joseph Payne Brennan; © 1966 by H.S.D. Publications, Inc.; reprinted by permission of the author.

'THE COST OF KENT CASTWELL' by Avram Davidson; © 1961 by H.S.D. Publications, Inc.; reprinted by permission of Kirby McCauley, Ltd.

'MY UNFAIR LADY' by Guy Cullingford; copyright 1958 by H.S.D. Publications, Inc.; reprinted by permission of the author.

'VACATION' by Mike Brett; © 1965 by H.S.D. Publications Inc.; reprinted by permission of Scott Meredith Literary Agency, Inc.

'A FLOWER FOR HER GRAVE' by Hilda Cushing; copyright H.S.D. Publications, Inc., 1969; reprinted by permission of the author.

CONTENTS

Career Man

by James Holding

Cardone looked at the tapestry. His eyes sharpened, his thin lips tightened. And he thought to himself, you never know. You really don't. Here I am in a little Hindu shop thousands of miles from home in the middle of this dust bowl called India, and all of a sudden I may be looking at the biggest heist of my entire career.

It was characteristic of Cardone that he used the word 'career' in his thoughts to cover the twenty-two years of his life that had started, inauspiciously enough, with muggings and petty burglaries, had proceeded to various grand larcenies committed while armed, and had ultimately ensconced him as a leading practitioner in that most respectable of criminal specialties, bank robbery. Cardone had no scruples, moral or ethical. He was proud of his record, so he called it a 'career'. It did not signify that his last caper, the robbery of a bank in a small Colorado town, had so nearly ended in his apprehension by the police that he had decided an extended trip abroad might provide a beneficial cooling-off period.

Aside from the slight change in the expression of his eyes and lips, no sign of his emotions showed as he stared through the glass at The Pride of India. Mr. Ganeshi Lall, standing at his shoulder, intoned proudly in excellent English, 'There are eighteen thousand jewels embroidered on that tapestry, sir. Emeralds, rubies, diamonds and sapphires, of course, as well as most of the semi-precious stones to be found in India. The tapestry was manufactured in our establishment, the gems sewn into the fabric by our own workmen. Fifty thousand working hours were involved. It demonstrates the fine craftmanship of Ganeshi Lall & Son.'

Cardone nodded, impressed. 'It does, indeed,' he said. 'The six-by-eight-foot tapestry was literally encrusted with gems. 'How much is it worth?'

'One million dollars. At least it is insured for that, you understand. When it was displayed at the World's Fair...'

Cardone interrupted him. 'And you have it hanging here in plain sight, protected only by this glass case, almost inviting larceny?'

'Mr. Lall smiled. 'Of course,' he said. 'It is a great attraction for tourists, naturally. But it is quite safe, please. A very complicated American burglar alarm safeguards it.'

'Cardone already knew that. The gold leaf of the burglar alarm laced the protective glass through which they gazed at the tapestry, but it was nice to have Mr. Lall, the owner of The Pride of India, admit it so readily. With a slight turn of his head, Cardone discovered where the connecting wires entered the room.

A score of other tourists had joined them now before The Pride of India. Mr. Lall was busy answering questions from awe-stricken gapers. Cardone, fumbling in his jacket pocket for a cigarette, drifted to the edge of the crowd, sauntered peacefully over to inspect a jade Buddha five yards away. As he withdrew the cigarette from his pocket, it escaped his fingers and fell to the floor near the base of the carved Buddha. Cardone leaned to pick it up. With one swift, beautifully-disguised movement, he used the little tool he had brought from his pocket with the cigarette to sever cleanly the burglar alarm wires that disappeared through the baseboard behind the statue.

It began on the veranda of Lauries Hotel the afternoon before.

Recently arrived in Agra by plane from Bombay, along with thirty other American tourists who wanted to see the Taj Mahal, Cardone registered at the hotel desk, washed up in his room, and was taking the first grateful sip of a cool gin sling on the veranda before dinner, when he felt eyes upon him. That curious sixth sense, so often developed in persons outside the law, warned him that someone had him under observation. He glanced around to locate the observer. All the little nerve ends in his wary body were erect and seeking.

The squatting dhoti-clad sellers of ivory, brass and marble curios who, with their wares, occupied most of the veranda space near him, were paying no attention to him. His fellow tourists, mostly female, chattered like temple monkeys around him, but a quick survey assured him that none was regarding him. Then he turned his head slightly toward the doorway of the hotel bar and encountered, with an impact almost physical, the eyes that were watching him.

They belonged to a tall, massively-built Hindu with brush-cut hair above a square brown solid face. He stood behind a pillar of the porch to Cardone's right, down three steps on the gravel driveway that bordered the veranda. Dressed in western clothes, his expression was open and candid, and the watching eyes were unusually dark, even for a Hindu. Then Cardone forgot the man's appearance in speculation as to why he was so intensely interested in an American tourist – a perfect stranger, but also, it must be admitted, a slightly hot bank robber at home.

When the Hindu realized Cardone was aware of his scrutiny, he smiled and approached, slipping up the three steps to the veranda gracefully, despite his bulk. 'Mr. Cardone?' he asked politely.

Cardone was startled. The guy knew his name. He set his drink down on the table very slowly. 'That's me,' he admitted coolly. 'What can I do for you?' Maybe the fellow had looked over his shoulder when he registered.

'I am Mirajkar Dass,' the man introduced himself with a little bow. 'Driver and guide. Would the gentleman permit me to show him the Taj Mahal and other Agra sights while in our city? Please?'

Cardone thought Mirajkar's eyes were signaling him, but he didn't know what. 'I'm with a tour,' he said brusquely, indicating the vociferous group nearby. 'We're taken care of, thanks.'

'A private guide, sir,' the man insisted gently, 'is much more satisfactory. I have a very nice American car, and I speak English very good.'

'I'm with a tour, buddy. We got a guide, and we see the sights in buses. Thanks just the same.'

Mirajkar refused to be brushed off. 'I've always admired your work, Mr. Cardone,' he said softly.

For an instant, Cardone froze in his chair, oblivious of the chattering tourists around him. Then he looked up at the tall Hindu and nodded reluctantly. 'Don't bother me now,' he said, 'but maybe you've got something with this private guide thing. Come to my room after dinner and we'll talk it over, okay?'

'Okay,' Mirajkar agreed instantly, a warm light of pleasure appearing momentarily in his dark eyes. 'After dinner, sir.' He unobtrusively withdrew to the driveway to take up his stand beside the porch pillar once more.

Does he know my room number too? Cardone wondered uneasily. He took a gulp of his gin sling, his thoughts running oddly on the fact that he really would enjoy seeing Agra on his own with his own guide, rather than in the company of all the tour members.

After having chicken curry for dinner that was so hot it put to shame the Mexican seasoning Cardone had sampled at home, he lit a cigarette and strolled to his room at the end of the hotel's ground floor colonade. The flickering electric bulbs along the arcade threw their light only a few feet to either side where it was hungrily swallowed up by the pitch darkness of the hotel's gardens. Cardone was an easy target to anyone concealed in that darkness, he was aware, but although he was small in stature and physically un-impressive, Cardone did not lack courage. His 'career' testified to that. He was calm and unhurried in his walk to his room; he even stopped once to take a long savoring breath of the dust-and-dung-scented air. The hand that inserted his key in the door was quite steady.

As the door opened under his hand, he felt a presence materialize behind him. When he switched on the light and turned to close the door, the Hindu was already inside the room.

Cardone, without preamble, said, 'How'd you know my name?'

Mirajkar shrugged. 'A college classmate of mine was your guide in Bombay last week. He telephoned me you were coming here.'

The big Hindu was a college man, it seemed. Cardone automatically fought against a feeling of inferiority that usually assailed him when talking to college graduates.

Cardone himself hadn't finished the eighth grade. But why should Mirajkar's pal telephone him that Cardone was coming to Agra? Just to tout him onto a possible customer for his guide's services? Not likely. Then why?

Pressing for information, Cardone asked, 'Why did he do that?'

'Telephone me you were coming? Because he thought you were the right man to help us with a little project we have here in Agra.'

'Wait a minute, buster. What's that mean?'

'He recognized you.'

'How could he do that?'

'He was in America getting his Master's degree several years ago, at the University of Colorado. He saw your photograph in the newspapers.'

'Me? He saw my picture in the papers? He was wrong. This is all a big fat mistake. Sorry, buddy.'

'No, Mr. Cardone. He remembered the picture very well. You were being questioned in a bank robbery case in Boulder. Everybody thought you were guilty, but nothing tangible could be proved.'

'You're so right it couldn't. I'm not completely stupid,' he said, 'even if I didn't go to college.'

'You are a very skilful thief,' Mirajkar said with an apologetic gesture of his hands that seemed to disassociate him from the blunt statement. 'My friend knew that. That's why he telephoned me.'

'I haven't made a score of any kind in India,' Cardone hastened to defend himself.

'Of course. That is what I have to offer you, sir, the opportunity to make a wonderful score by helping us.'

Cardone breathed out cigarette smoke, relieved. 'So sit down,' he invited, waving a hand. 'I'll turn on the air conditioning.'

What could be worth stealing in this jerk town?

As though reading his mind, Mirajkar said in his pleasant baritone, 'The Pride of India. It is here in Agra. And it is easily accessible to one of your experience.'

'What's the Pride of India?' Cardone asked.

The Hindu told him in some detail.

'A tapestry!' Cardone protested when he had finished. 'Six

feet by four! What if it's covered with ice? We'd never be able to move it out of Agra once we had it. It's too big.'

'Permit me, Mr. Cardone. My friend and I have given a great deal of thought to that. It is another reason why you can be of such help to us.'

'Goody,' Cardone said sardonically.

'Yes. When you have stolen the tapestry, we will cut the best of the precious stones from the fabric. They are all unset, and not so very large as to be easily recognizable except in India.'

'Well, that's an idea,' Cardone said. 'Then what?'

'Then you smuggle them out of India in your luggage when you go home. With due caution, you realize cash for them in America. I am sure you have connections there to accommodate you in a matter of this kind?'

'I know a few people,' Cardone admitted cautiously. He was beginning to feel his heart beats quicken a little. 'What's this Pride of India likely to split out at?'

'We estimate a minimum of a million and a quarter rupees.'

'What's that in dollars?'

'Almost a quarter of a million.' Mirajkar allowed this succulent figure to hang in the air between them for a moment before he continued. 'That tapestry is insured for five million rupees, Mr. Cardone, but that is the estimated value of the tapestry as it is. If we remove the jewels and accept a fifty to seventy-five percent loss on their true value, by reason of having to dispose of them surreptitiously, we should still realize a quarter of a million dollars.'

Cardone said, 'That's important sugar. Split three ways, eh?'

'Split two ways. Half for you, half for us. After all, you will do most of the work.'

'That's for sure. Otherwise you'd never proposition me.'

'Does it sound attractive to you?'

'It has possibilities. What did you say your name is?'

'Mirajkar Dass.'

'I'll call you Dass,' Cardone said. 'That other name's a laugh.'

Mirajkar bowed, smiling. 'As you wish, sir. The Pride of India hangs behind a glass case in the shop of Ganeshi Lall &

Son on Mahatma Gandhi Road, right near this hotel. Almost every American tourist who comes to Agra goes into the shop to see it.'

'How hard will the store be to crack?'

'Not difficult for you. No night guards are left, if that is what you mean, and you are good with locks, we have heard.'

Cardone was modest. 'Not too bad,' he said.

'But there are burglar alarms. That is mainly why we need you. You must have had a wide experience with them.

Cardone grinned. 'I'm the best little alarm-gimmicker in the business. But I want to see the layout before we try anything.'

'Good,' Mirajkar said. 'Tomorrow you can see it without suspicion. All your group will probably see it. As your private guide, I will take you there when there is a good crowd. You can look at the door locks and the burglar alarm arrangements, perhaps prepare things for an attempt tomorrow night?'

'We'll see. Anyway, you're hired as my guide and driver.'

'I shall try to give satisfactory service.'

'Yeah, but wait a minute. You're going too fast, Dass. You say I'm going to take these jewels to America, fence them for cash, then send you your share. Is that right?'

'That is right.'

'You'll trust me to take the stuff and send your cut?'

'We must, Mr. Cardone. It is all we can do. We cannot gimmick (is that the word you used?) the burglar alarm at Lall's without you. Even if we could, we could not dispose of the gems in India. They are known here. When the tapestry is stolen, the announcement of its theft will alert every jeweler in India. So we *must* trust you. You can see the point. No?'

'What makes you think I won't keep the whole bundle for myself once I get to America?'

Mirajkar said seriously, 'There is honor among thieves, is there not?'

Cardone nodded solemnly, then he probed a little deeper. 'What is it with you two guys, Dass, that you're getting into the heist racket? You're both college men, aren't you? You got brains. You got good jobs as guides...'

Mirajkar interrupted him indignantly. 'Good jobs! There

are no good jobs in India. We are guides and chauffeurs to tourists, that is all! And we must have college education to be eligible even for that!

'Most of our income is in tips from rich Americans and, forgive me, most of you are not generous. We will not live like this for the rest of our lives. We are educated men, worthy of more dignified treatment, and we shall get it when we have a quarter million rupees apiece.' The soft eyes blazed and the big hands clenched in unmistakable earnestness.

'Okay, okay, Dass,' said Cardone, feeling infinitely better about his own abbreviated education. 'Don't make a production of it, pal. I see what you mean.' He lit another cigarette and offered the Hindu one. They smoked in companionable silence for a time. Cardone's mind was busy. At last he said to Mirajkar, 'Tell me about this alarm system.'

That's how it happened that Cardone visited the shop of Ganeshi Lall the next afternoon. Before he left it, he thoroughly nullified the system of burglar alarms that protected The Pride of India. Lall's boast of a very complicated American burglar alarm proved, upon expert inspection, to have been a major over-assessment of an almost primitive arrangement. Inconspicuously and skill-fully, therefore, during ostensible tourist shopping in the Lall showroom, Cardone had arranged that the Pride of India's alarm system, when switched on at closing time that night, would appear as efficient as usual but would fail to function. Even the door alarms, meant to alert the police in their headquarters a block away in case of any attempt to enter Lall's shop, were put out of commission with an ease that Cardone found laughable.

When he entered Mirajkar's automobile, waiting for him on the dusty drive before Lall's emporium, he was still chuckling. To the anxious question in Dass' eyes, he answered, 'It was a breeze, Dass. We'll be able to lift the rug tonight without even working up a sweat.'

Mirajkar put his car in gear and pulled away from Lall's. 'We will now visit the tomb of Akbar the Great at Sikandra,' he said in his best guide's voice, then added in his own, 'You like the tapestry?'

'Terrific, Dass.'

'You believe the project worthwhile, then.' The car rattled and shook as Mirajkar guided it northward toward the Delhi Gate. 'How long do you estimate it will take you to steal the tapestry tonight, sir?'

Cardone said blandly, 'Portal to portal, not more than five minutes. I'll be inside the shop in two, have the tapestry out of its frame in two more, and be back outside in one more. Five minutes, Dass. I've already done all the hard work.'

Mirajkar nodded, excitement gripping him. 'My friend in Bombay was right. You are a professional, Mr. Cardone. I respect you for it.'

'It don't pay to get mixed up with amateurs,' Cardone said. He felt expansive, sure of success. He basked a little in the Hindu's admiration.

'Five minutes,' Mirajkar repeated. 'Then we can do it on our way to the Taj Mahal tonight and never be missed. There is full moon tonight, and all tourists must see the Taj by moonlight. Your tour members will go in their bus. I shall drive you. But we will stop for five minutes at Lall's on the way, you understand. We will leave the hotel when your tour does, and arrive at the Taj at the same time. Five minutes we can spare easily by taking a short cut. You see?'

'Okay, you're the doctor. That sounds like enough of an alibi for me, but I want to be sure of a safe place to cut the ice out of the rug, and a foolproof way to smuggle the loose stones out of India.'

'Both are easily supplied,' Mirajkar said. 'We will cut the gems from the tapestry at the Taj itself, immediately after we steal the tapestry.'

'At the Taj?' Cardone had already viewed the magnificent tomb of Mumtaz Mahal by sunrise that morning. 'You're nuts! It's a public place. It'll be dark. We'll be surrounded by romantic tourists.'   'I have a key to one of the minarets, Mr. Cardone, moulded long ago in the hope of future usefulness. The minarets have been closed to the public for years. Many people used to commit suicide by casting themselves down from them, inspired by the romantic love and tragic end of Shahjahan and Mumtaz, no doubt. So we shall be very private at the top of a minaret, with no interruptions.'

'Light?'

'Moonlight will serve, sir. Full moon tonight, as I said.'

'What about the smuggling bit?'

'All planned, Mr. Cardone. I estimate the gems we shall cut from the tapestry will be fairly bulky, even though we take merely the better ones. Perhaps a two-quart measure might hold them. Do you agree?'

'So?'

'I have prepared three wooden carvings for you to take home from India as souvenirs. They are carvings of the three wives of Lord Shiva, the Destroyer – Parvati, the goddess of domestic happiness; Durga, the goddess of power; Kali, the goddess of blood and war.'

'Never mind the theology, Dass,' said Cardone. 'What about the carvings?'

'These statues are common tourist souvenirs, turned out by the hundreds here, but our three are slightly different. They are hollow, with a screw-on base for each that cunningly fits into a crease in the fold of each lady's garment. I guarantee the joint to be undetectable by any customs official. The jewels will be placed inside the three carvings, stuffed in solidly and packed with cotton.' Mirajkar smiled, turning his head to look at Cardone in the back seat. 'Good?'

'Okay,' said Cardone. 'Where are they?'

'Under that lap rob beside you, sir.'

Cardone examined the carvings. 'Pretty clever, Dass. These ought to do it.' He lit a cigarette. 'What happens to the rug after we've cut off the ice?'

'It stays in the minaret of the Taj. No one ever goes there now.'

That seemed to cover it. Cardone leaned back in his seat as they passed the lunatic asylum on the Sikandra road and relaxed. The eyes of his body saw mango, neem, tamarind and acacia trees march by, enlivened by flitting mynah birds, crows, flocks of green parrots, and vultures perched patiently on gnarled limbs, waiting for something to die; but the eyes of his mind beheld only double handfuls of diamonds, rubies, emeralds and sapphires. Cardone touched absently with a forefinger the bulge under his arm where his gun lay, and looking at the back of Mirajkar's head, his thin lips curved in what passed with him for a smile.

That night, it all went like clockwork. Waving gaily to the busload of his fellow tourists as they started out from the hotel at nine o'clock, Cardone and his driver-guide, Marajkar, were already parking the car in the wide parking lot before the Taj gate by the time the bus arrived. No one suspected that they had stopped for five minutes before the darkened shop of Ganeshi Lall, and that The Pride of India was now in Mirajkar's car. No one thought anything of the fact that Mirajkar, as a private guide who knew the foibles of tourists extremely well, was carrying an automobile lap robe over his arm when they left the car, in case his 'gentleman' might want to sit for a while on the damp grass, or a marble pool coping, and contemplate in awed silence the most magnificent tomb in the world. No one missed them when Cardone and Mirajkar wandered slowly down the cypress-lined mall past the silent fountains before the Taj, loudly admiring its ethereal beauty in the moonlight, and disappeared.

The blinking oil lamps carried by the Taj Mahal guards cast weird shadows inside the soaring arch of the entrance and on the marble platform nearby, where daytime tourists obtained their mosque slippers to prevent their infidel feet from violating the sanctity of the tomb.

The minaret to which Mirajkar had a key was on the northeast corner of the enormous platform, behind the Taj. Its slender finger pointed to the sky directly above the river bank. They approached it carefully in the moonlight from the side avoiding the front entrance of the Taj entirely.

Mirajkar fumbled in the shadowed side of the galleried obelisk to get the small iron door open. Cardone looked upward. At the top of the minaret, he saw the open, pillared gallery that crowned it. Then he looked sidelong toward the entrance of the Taj, now out of sight, where the nearest guard would be, noting with satisfaction that it was almost a hundred yards away. He whispered, nevertheless, when he spoke to Mirajkar.

'This is real privacy, Dass. You couldn't have done better.'

'Thanks. I think it will serve well enough.'

The door came open with a loud rasp of metal against marble which Mirajkar ignored calmly. 'No one could possibly hear it,' he explained when Cardone inadvertently winced.

They entered the narrow door at the foot of the minaret. 'Go on up,' the Hindu told Cardone. He shifted the rug over his arm to a more comfortable position. 'To the top.'

'Okay. Need any help with the tapestry? It must weigh a hundred pounds.'

'No, thanks, sir. I can manage it.' Mirajkar patted the concealing lap robe fondly.

Cardone began to climb the narrow spiral stairway of marble inside the minaret. He counted the steps almost unconsciously, and was surprised when the total came to a hundred and sixty-four. He was puffing when he emerged into the small circular chamber at the top. Between the graceful columns that walled the gallery, he could see the moonlit Jumna River below him curving away across the plain to the north; to the west were the clustered lights and houses of Agra, huddled around the massive dark walls of the Fort; to the south the huge, moon-bright domes of the Taj Mahal were almost on a level with his eyes. The view was breathtaking.

Cardone gave it only a quick glance, however. He turned as Mirajkar labored up out of the dark stairwell behind him. 'Bring it over where we can see, Dass. Put the rug down on the floor here in the moonlight and we'll start to operate.' He laughed. 'Got your fingernail scissors?'

Mirajkar nodded. He put the lap robe, and what it concealed, carefully down on the floor without unfolding it. 'I have them in my pocket. It shouldn't take us long.' He reached into his jacket pocket.

Cardone said, 'Might as well give me the car keys too.'

'The car keys?' Mirajkar looked at Cardone in surprise.

'Yeah,' said Cardone, his voice amused. 'You won't be needing them any more. I will, however.'

The Hindu drew in his breath with a faint hiss. Instead of manicure scissors with which to cut the gems free of the tapestry, Cardone held in his hand a gun fitted with a silencer. It was pointing unwaveringly at Mirajkar's heart.

'But Mr. Cardone, we are partners in this!' The guide ran out of words and was silent, his eyes glinting big in the moonlight.

'We *were* partners, Dass. But who needs you now?'

The tall Hindu looked briefly toward the dark stairwell. He said nothing.

'Too late to scram,' Cardone said. 'You understand why I have to kill you, don't you?'

'No. You could get to America and merely keep all the proceeds from the jewels yourself. Why kill me?'

'Because I can take it from here without your help. As a professional, I wouldn't want to leave an eyewitness to a heist of mine behind me, would I?'

'I suppose not. You said it does not pay to get mixed up with amateurs.'

'You got it now, pal, and you're an amateur.' Cardone laughed softly. 'I've got to hand it to you, though, for lining this caper up – right down to the hollow carvings I can use to smuggle the ice out.'

'They aren't here,' Mirajkar reminded him.

'They're in the car, and that's where I'm going after I cut the stuff off the rug. Let's have the keys, buddy boy.'

Slowly Mirajkar handed them over. 'If you shoot me, someone will hear you. You will be trapped in this tower.'

'I cased the minaret before we came up. It's too far away, especially with this.' He touched the silencer on his pistol barrel.

'My friend in Bombay will know you killed me.'

'I'll take that chance. What's he know, anyhow? Nothing. I'll be in Paris before he even knows you're dead.'

'Paris?'

'Or someplace else. You don't think I'd go back home with this loot, do you? I'm hot there right now.'

'You promised to, and send us our share.'

'Yeah, that's right. Honor among thieves, wasn't it? Even if you're a college man, Dass, your I.Q. is for the birds. I'm flying out of here tomorrow morning – for somewhere, and I'll leave your car right in its regular place in front of the hotel. Nobody will even know you're dead, sucker. They'll be worrying about the Pride of India being gone. No time to wonder about a missing native guide.'

'I see,' said Mirajkar slowly. 'You shoot me. You cut the jewels off the tapestry there,' he nodded toward the lap robe, 'go out and put them into the carvings, drive my car back to the hotel and leave Agra tomorrow.'

'That's about it. You got any better ideas?'

'Yes. Let me help you cut the jewels off before you shoot me. It will save valuable time for you. The Taj grounds close at ten o'clock, you know. You may not finish the job in time alone.'

Cardone cast a quick glance at his wristwatch. 'I'll make it, Dass. Don't worry.' His finger tightened on the trigger of the gun. Mirajkar stood motionless.

'Goodbye, sucker,' Cardone said. 'No hard feelings.' He pulled the trigger.

The Hindu leaned slowly over toward the lap robe on the floor. When he straighted up again, he held the robe loosely in his hand. There was nothing on the floor where it had been.

'The Pride of India is not here, Cardone,' he said. His tone contained the barest suggestion of contempt. 'You have made what you call a big fat mistake.'

Cardone hardly heard him. He was looking accusingly at the gun in his hand, genuine shock in his eyes. 'What is this?' he said unbelievingly. He pointed the barrel at Dass and pulled the triger six times in rapid succession. The clicks of the hammer falling on empty chambers were like small deprecatory sounds a man makes with his tongue and teeth when he is overwhelmingly frustrated.

'Yesterday,' said Mirajkar, 'I was one of the drivers that brought your party from the airport to the hotel. I also helped to distribute your luggage to the proper rooms. I placed your bag in your room, sir, while you were registering. It had your name on it, so I took a quick glance inside and found your gun. Knowing I might have dealings with you later, if fortune favored me, I took the liberty of removing the cartridge – just in case.' He smiled in the moonlight, his teeth appearing big and white in the dark face. 'It seems I was wise to do so.'

Cardone grunted. 'This was before you braced me on the veranda?'

'Certainly.'

'I take it back, Dass. You're no amateur.'

Mirajkar bowed. 'Thank you. From you, it is a compliment.'

'Where's The Pride of India? Still in the car?'

'Yes. I thought it could do no harm to take precautions, so I slipped it out from under the lap robe just as we left.'

'You're pretty sharp, Dass. I'll give you that. You've played this whole thing pretty cool for a foreigner. So now we start over, is that it?'

'Not quite, Mr. Cardone. As you so admirably phrased it, who needs you now? You stole The Pride of India for me, handling the burglar alarm systems very professionally. To my shame, I know nothing about electricity.'

'Yeah, I know. You're just an amateur.'

'Exactly, sir. But now that The Pride of India is in my hands, your usefulness ends. I fear.'

'How do you figure: You still can't dispose of those jewels off the tapestry without me, pal. You said yourself it was impossible in India.'

'Quite true.'

'So?' Cardone tried to sound more confident than he felt. He fiddled with the empty gun in his hand, damning himself for a fool for not checking it when he'd strapped the holster on that morning. 'You'll be needing me to fence the stuff for you. Right?'

'Not right. I never intended to cut the gems from the tapestry, Mr. Cardone.'

The American suddenly felt trapped. Too many surprises were coming at him all at once. He raised his eyebrows. 'Then why the hollowed-out statues and all that jazz?'

'Merely additional touches to assure you of my good faith.'

'Good faith!' Cardone laughed with a high, hysterical giggle.

'Let me explain, sir. My friend in Bombay who told me about you is in reality my cousin. He is the son of my uncle who works for the insurance company that insures The Pride of India for five million rupees.'

Cardone's shoulders slumped.

'When The Pride of India is reported stolen, the insurance company will generously pay a ten percent reward for its return, with no questions asked. I happen to know that, because my uncle's company paid that amount on a previous occasion.' Mirajkar coughed.

'For the return of The Pride of India? It's been heisted before?'

'Once before; this is the second time. Without undue pride I may tell you, sir, that on both occasions the theft was arranged by me.'

'You collected the reward before?'

Mirajkar bowed.

'And will collect it again this time?'

'Yes. A quarter of a million rupees for my cousin and me.'

'I'm sorry – sorry I called you an amateur.'

The Hindu shrugged. 'My cousin does the difficult part – selecting professional help for us from among his tourist groups in Bombay, as he selected you, Mr. Cardone. Of course, we must pay a small percentage to my uncle with the insurance company for his cooperation.'

Cardone thought, Amateurs! But this time he didn't speak it aloud.

Mirajkar said, 'It is too bad you underestimated us, sir. But take comfort, you will die in the most beautiful tourist attraction in the world.' Curiously enough, Mirajkar's voice held a note of genuine emotion when he spoke of the Taj.

'Die?'

'What else can you expect? You yourself said it is unprofessional to leave a living witness behind you.'

That's when Cardone gave up hope. He reversed the gun in his hand and hurled it savagely at the Hindu's head, but with a negligent lifting of the lap robe in his hand, the Hindu caught the gun in its wooden folds. It dropped harmlessly to the floor with a small metallic crash.

Mirajkar reached then for the American. There was no escape for the smaller man. The Hindu towered over him. His arms were like steel ropes around Cardone's body. He forced Cardone toward the pillars of the tiny gallery.

'You will be a suicide, sir,' he said into Cardone's ear with amusement. 'I shall tell the authorities when they find you that, as your guide and driver for the past two days, I have heard you speaking with deep despair of an unrequited love – the great love of your life. I shall tell them you came away from America to get over this passion of yours for another man's wife, but that your emotions must have overcome you when you saw by moonlight the ineffable beauty of the Taj Mahal where lie the remains of history's most romantic couple. And alas, while I waited for you, at your request, in the gardens below, you must have done as so many star-crossed lovers have done before you: leaped to your death from a minaret gallery. I may even raise the alarm over your absence at closing time myself.' He forced Cardone to look downward over the gallery's edge. 'As your official guide, sir, I can inform you that the distance you will fall is exactly one hundred sixty-two and a quarter feet.'

Cardone struggled helplessly in the big Hindu's grip. Mirajkar casually offered the crowning insult by holding Cardone with only one hand while his other dipped into Cardone's pocket for the car keys only recently surrendered to him.

'It will be readily explained,' he continued to speak remorselessly, 'how you could gain entrance to a locked minaret to stage your act of self-destruction. Were you not a professional burglar? One of the best? A criminal to whom opening a little door like this would be merest child's play? I bid you goodbye, Mr. Cardone. And our deepest thanks for your professional assistance.'

Almost negligently, he brought the edge of one stiffened hand against Cardone's Adam's apple, effectively paralyzing his vocal chords, choking off the shout for help that was bubbling in the American's throat. Then he quickly pushed Cardone over the gallery's edge between two of the columns.

Falling, Cardone saw the black-and-white marble squares of the Taj Mahal platform rushing up to meet him like a pinwheeling, demented chess board. He made no sound. He was voiceless. But he was conscious, for a split second before his shattered body became a dark blot on the moon-washed marble, of an obscure sense of satisfaction that it had taken a college man to best him in his chosen profession.

A Flower in Her Hair

by Pauline C. Smith

'While you're here, I s'pose I better take you over to see Aunt Abbie.'

'Aunt Abbie?' questioned the girl. 'Who is she?'

'Well, she ain't really an aunt, but she's some relation...' Melinda's voice trailed off as her memory attempted to locate the offshoot on the family tree that was Aunt Abbie. 'Bein' my second cousin, I guess she's pretty fur removed from you.' She gazed at her visitor uncertainly, then her eyes turned resolute. 'But she's blood kin, so you should see her.'

'Why?' The girl was growing impatient of distant family ties woven to strangle her in this strange country of her mother's.

Melinda bustled. 'She's the record keeper. Got second sight too.'

'When do we have to go?' Tradition and folklore were losing their piquancy.

Again Melinda looked doubtfully upon the city-bred frailty of her guest. 'Well, it's quite a piece. Rough ground. But I guess we better get over there today, you're leavin' so soon.'

The girl sighed, mentally ticking off the hours left to her here.

In the hot sun she followed in the wake of Melinda's angular maturity, which plowed a furrow through weeds and thistle, over boudler-strewn hillsides bare of trees and bristling with prickly growth that offered no protection from the beating heat.

At last, Melinda turned to look at the girl behind her. 'We better stop and rest awhile, I guess.' She eased her bulk down carefully, watching her companion slump to the ground. 'Tired, ain'tcha?'

The girl nodded.

'I shoulda remembered you ain't used to this kind o' country. Your face sure is flushed.'

The girl thrust out a lower lip to blow cooling air across her cheeks.

'You redheads sunburn, don'tcha?'

Again the girl nodded.

Melinda turned reflective. 'Don't know that there ever was a redhead in the family before...'

'My father had auburn hair.'

'Oh. I never seen him. Your ma's hair was black's a raven's wing.'

'I remember.'

Melinda heaved herself to her broad feet. 'Might's well get goin' if we want to get back by sundown. Ain't fur now.' She pointed. 'Just up the hill and over to the ridge. See it in a little bit.'

The cabin finally appeared in the distance, like a lookout on the rim.

Staring curiously, the girl asked, 'Is that it?'

'That's it. Aunt Abbie's lived there now goin' on fifty year.'

'How old is she?'

They had reached the summit. The cabin squatted beneath bowed trees that held hands over its roof.

'She must be over seventy now. Spry, though. Spry's a chicken.' Melinda took a sidelong glance at her weary companion. 'Climbs these hills like a mountain goat when she's a mind to.'

The girl knew even a gentle thrust when she felt one. Her mouth tightened. 'Well,' she said flatly, 'I just hope she's spry enough to get me a nice cold drink of water.'

'She'll have grapejuice. Always keep a pitcherful down in the cave.'

The girl paused to stare over the ridge and into the gorge below. She backed up, trembling. 'Are she sure she's home?'

'Aunt Abbie? Oh, sure. She don't go noplace. Always busy,' Melinda said with certainty as she stepped through a broken gate and up a path hemmed in by weed-choked flowers.

The door was open. Melinda poked her head through. 'Aunt Abbie,' she shrieked. Behind her, the girl stumbled over a claw hammer at the sill. She kicked it aside and into the weeds.

'Aunt Abbie,' shouted Melinda again.

'Yes, yes, yes. I'm a-comin'.'

Erupting from the shadows, peering into the sunlight, Aunt Abbie strained forward. As Melinda had said, she was spry, as spry as a taut steel spring. Her meager nose projected itself before her. Her dark eyes were lodestones and her mouth an iron bar.

'Oh, it's you, Melinda. Who's that you got with you?'

Melinda stepped aside to give the girl an abrupt shove into the room. 'This here's Marty's girl. She's been stoppin' with us a coupla days.'

Aunt Abbie shifted relationships through her mind. 'Marty's girl.' Inspecting her, she reached forth a clawlike hand with a feather touch. The girl drew minutely away. 'Come in. Come in and set down.'

Sidling into the room, the girl backed to a chair, feeling the slick, wooden arms of it with her fingertips. As she sat on the edge of the broken cane seat, Aunt Abbie stood before her. Again the claws reached out. 'Marty's girl. Such pretty red hair.' Talons hovered over the girl's shining head, suspended there. 'Such awful pretty red hair.' Aunt Abbie turned to Melinda. 'Did you ever see such pretty red hair?'

Melinda shook her head. 'Can't say I ever did. Guess I never seen any red hair in this family before. She says she got it from her pa.'

The girl shrank, her eyes moving cautiously from Aunt Abbie to the objects in the room – cluttered and stacked souvenirs – a chaos of remembrance.

'She's thirsty,' suggested Melinda.

Aunt Abbie took another covetous look at the flaming hair. 'Such a pretty red. Yes, Melinda. I'll fetch some grapejuice.' She scuttled from the room.

The girl heard a door slam, quick, staccato footsteps descending.

The room grew brighter as her eyes adjusted. 'So much stuff,' she murmured.

'Aunt Abbie keeps everything,' Melinda explained

proudly. 'All the family records too. Them rugs she made from relations' clothes.'

As Melinda gestured with humble admiration, the girl looked down upon the oblongs, circles, hooked and braided, crocheted and cross-stitched; utilization of the rags of memory, placed in precision like an army, white pine boards between the battalions.

'She made all them samplers too.'

The girl raised her eyes to stare at the walls with their exquisite needlework. Each square of cloth threaded with a MAY HE REST IN PEACE or derivative. 'When they die,' explained Melinda, 'she stiches 'em up.'

The girl shuddered, drowned in her own morbid fascination. Her eyes fixed themselves on the bright colors of death.

'I'll try and get Aunt Abbie to show you the wreath,' Melinda whispered, her eyes rolling, her breast swelling beneath coarse cotton, her large spare body quivering with anticipation.

The girl offered no answering interest, intent only upon the sound of scrambling footsteps as they returned. Her every thought, every desire, was to get away from here, from the saffron face of Aunt Abbie, her nimble tread, the heavy cup pushed so gently, ever so insidiously, into her hand.

The girl sipped the cold, dark liquid.

'Good, ain't it?' prodded Melinda.

She nodded with a faint smile and a thread of purple parting her lips. Stiffly then, with eyes averted, she placed the half-full cup on the marble-topped table at her side.

Aunt Abbie stood lightly on a hooked memorial, watching her. 'Your ma had black hair.' She turned to Melinda. 'Remember how dark Marty's hair was?'

Melinda nodded. 'I thought maybe you'd show us your you-know-what...'

Aunt Abbie looked speculatively at the girl. She extended a hand, fingers curved, almost touching the bright hair. 'I'll fetch it.'

The girl was deep in the chair now, feeling the stiff, jagged ends of broken cane. Her stomach curled; streaks of cold hunched her shoulders. Sluggishly, she gazed out at the shaft of sunshine in the doorway.

'Oh, the book of records too,' called Melinda, leaning forward as Aunt Abbie returned to squat before the girl.

Carefully, Aunt Abbie laid the large gilt frame on a braided rug. She opened a book upon her knees.

'That,' explained Melinda, 'is the family record. The first part shows the birthings. The last part, the dyings.'

Aunt Abbie flipped pages, her sepia fingers fondling the last of them, clean and unwritten. 'How old are you, my dear?'

'Twenty -four.'

'Just twenty-four. Well, well. Your ma lived to be ... let's see ...' She leafed back. 'Thirty-two. Your branch of the family always did go young. Your pa ain't in here. He wan't kin.'

'Dad died last year.'

'You're all alone?'

'Well, yes ...'

'Except for us.'

The girl was hazily displeased with the tie-in. 'I'm just passing through here,' she said in minor revolt, 'on my way home. To the coast,' she added, feeling the necessity of identity, a longing for familiarity.

'Well, well, well,' Aunt Abbie crooned absently. Her mind seemed to wander as her eyes studied the girl. 'Well,' and she smiled, her lips sucking her teeth briskly. 'So you want to see the wreath?'

'Wreath?'

'The hair wreath.' Aunt Abbie placed the book on the floor and picked up the oval gilt frame. Its curves caught the beams of light from the doorway. She held it up against her knees, her fingers holding it in place. Steadily, she watched the girl.

The girl stared down and into a circlet of flowers painstakingly woven against the linen background. Twined into the floral hoop bloomed the white of cherry blossom, the gray of cactus spine, yellow daisies, brown iris, ashen lilies, goldenrod ...

Aunt Abbie bent her head, her liver-colored claw pointing out a portion of the wreath. 'See them? Them are black-eyes Susans. The centers come straight from your ma's hair. Pretty, ain't they?' The finger caressed the glossy black.

'My mother's *hair?*' The girl drew back, held her breath and allowed her face to blank out in utter disbelief.

'This here's made of hair. Didn't you know?'

The girl stared glassily at this incredible woman and her absurd handwork. She felt the sharp gouge of broken cane and the hard rungs of the chair against her back.

'It's got hair in it from every one of the family that's passed on.'

Melinda hitched closer, tipping her head as she gazed proudly down upon the wreath. 'Ain't it pretty now? Ain't it just elegant?' She shook her head with wonder. 'How she does it, I'll never know – all them fine hairs, the little bitty stitches. I wouldn't never have the patience.'

'You mean that's hair?' The girl clung to the arms of the chair because here was substance, here reality. 'Human hair? All of it?'

Aunt Abbie nodded, pleased. 'Just the family though,' she qualified with dignity. 'I wa'nt never one to fool with any that ain't kin.'

'And all those people are dead?'

Rising, Aunt Abbie leaned the frame against a table and stepped back to view it. 'That's how I keep 'em. It's a kind of memorial. Shows my respect, sort of.'

The girl stared at her, then back to the wreath. Her lips stretched, her nostrils flared.

'See?' Aunt Abbie's long finger pointed. 'I ain't got that rose in yet.' Reflectively, she gazed at the girl in the chair. 'I just got the rose left.'

The empty spot severed the circle like a break in a wedding ring. Outlines of rose petals had been sketched upon the linen. 'It's all that's left. Once I get that in, the wreath'll be done.'

The room began to swing, the wreath whirled concentrically, wreath within wreath, circle upon circle. Heat held the girl's body; chill released it. She placed an uncertain hand before her eyes. 'I'm a little sick,' she whispered weakly. Attempting to rise, she stumbled, and was caught in Melinda's strong but gentle grasp.

'She's a city girl,' she faintly heard Melinda apologize. 'She ain't used to the walk we took. We'll lay her on your cot, Aunt Abbie.'

She felt herself half-dragged, half-carried, through rolling blackness.

Melinda stepped from the sleeproom while Aunt Abbie tarried to stroke the shining hair on the pillow. Melinda paused in thought.

'She's a pretty sick girl. Too much, sun, maybe. Her skin looks kinda green, don't it?'

'Such pretty, pretty red hair,' said Aunt Abbie.

'Could be...' Melinda hesitated, absorbed now with a problem, beset by it and confused, 'could be I best go home alone and get Tom to come back with the truck and fetch her.' She looked upon Aunt Abbie for confirmation. 'She couldn't never walk through them hills again the way she –'

'You do that.' Aunt Abbie's decision was immediate and definite. She urged Melinda to the door, through it, and out into the sunshine. 'There ain't no hurry now. Not a mite of it. I'll tend to the girl. Don't you worry on it. I'll see she gets a nice long sleep.'

Without a single backward glance, Melinda walked over the boulders in the setting sun. Familiar with Aunt Abbie's competent hands and second sight, she felt a sense of accomplishment. Hadn't Aunt Abbie cured Old Opal of the jumps? And predicted the death of little Junie May? Nobody believed her that time, the baby being so fat and rosy-like. But lo and behold! Junie May died like *that!* Melinda, in recollection, chopped the air with her hand. That child's hair turned into the brightest yellow buttercups of them all.

When Tom arrived at near-dark, Melinda told him, 'There ain't no rushin' hurry. Aunt Abbie'll take care of the girl good. It's best we don't unsettle her rest tonight. We'll fetch her first thing in the mornin' though, so's she can catch her train.'

At daybreak, Melinda was pleased to relax on the seat of the truck. She spread her dress down over her thighs and leaned back against the wooden brace. The trip to Aunt Abbie's didn't take long this way, through dust-streaked fennel and the cool clear dawn.

'We'll fetch her right home so's she can pack up. It sure makes a girl puny to raise her up in the city. You wouldn't think that a bit of walk like that would get her ailin', now, would you? She's a sweet little thing, though, even if she ain't healthy. I've growed real fond on her.'

Aunt Abbie's cabin crouched in the shadow of the trees, a dreary and somnolent recluse. Melinda walked around it to the open door. She kicked a hammer from the sill into the weeds, and bent over to pick up a pocket mirror from the warped floor.

Inside, Aunt Abbie formed a pale sickle of absorption in the shadows, intent upon her needle, the gilt frame propped before her.

'How is she?' called Melinda.

Aunt Abbie turned slowly to peer through the gloom. 'How's who?'

'Why, Marty's girl, Aunt Abbie. She got to ailin' while we was vistin' yesterday. Remember?'

Aunt Abbie's mind seemed to reach back into all the yesterdays where it groped, fumbled, poked and pried. 'Oh, the redhead.' She turned back to her work and, with great care, slid her needle into the linen, the copper-red strand glinting against the half-finished rose. 'Well now, Melinda, did I tell you I seen death on that girl?'

Melinda clutched her heart and knew sudden terror. Then she rocked back to awe and veneration. 'You see that, Aunt Abbie? Like you seen it in Junie May?' Melinda was hypnotized by the shine of a wondrous second sight.

'Just the same,' said Aunt Abbie nodding. 'Just the same,' and took another stitch.

'You mean she's dead now, Aunt Abbie?'

'She's dead now.'

Aunt Abbie's words impaled Melinda's mind, to send her glance, slant-eyed, around the shadows of the room, searching out, yet sliding from the girl's departed soul.

It was then Melinda discovered the mirror in her hand – the mirror she had found on the porch. With reverence, she placed it, clear as a circular pond, upon the marble-topped table. She felt a moment's sharp grief for Marty's girl, quickly followed by respect for Aunt Abbie's ever-accurate prognostications. Melinda's breast was full of sorrow and it almost burst with pride.

With humility, Melinda took a step closer to the wreath. The rose had begun to take form. Bright and shining, under Aunt Abbie's able fingers.

'Where is she?' asked Melinda in hushed tones. 'Did you lay her out on your cot, Aunt Abbie?'

'She went walkin' to death, Melinda.' Aunt Abbie turned from her work and pierced Melinda with eyes that held the gift of knowledge. 'Some folk do that, Melinda. They go walkin' out to meet their death. Marty's girl went out to meet hers and tumbled right over into the gorge.'

Melinda could see it – the girl with outstretched arms – the gorge a black and yawning mouth.

'She's there *now*?' Melinda asked.

'Right down in the gorge. A broken flower.' Aunt Abbie returned to the wreath.

Melinda watched the bright hair snake through linen. She was fully aware that Aunt Abbie never snipped a live lock. Never. How many times had she observed Aunt Abbie's assistance to the dying? The mirror held patiently near to parted lips until no further fog clouded the surface. *Then* came the slash of scissors, and an aster grew upon the wreath, a russet chrysanthemum – now a rose.

Melinda's sorrowful, pride-filled mind knew perplexity. If Marty's girl had walked to death, had toppled over the rim and dropped deep in the gorge to meet it, how had aunt Abbie gone through the rites, those never-changing rites of the mirror, the slash of blades and the lock of hair?

Melinda retreated a reluctant step.

How?

Melinda's mind groped for understanding through its fog of indecision. Aunt Abbie was spry, spry as a mountain goat, but Melinda hadn't known she was spry enough to spring up the sheer face of the gorge – with scissors, hair and a mirror in her hand.

Melinda heaved a final sigh of acceptance. She guessed she was, though. Aunt Abbie, with her second sight and her talent for keeping the record, could do most anything, Melinda guessed.

'That's a mighty pretty rose,' she said at last.

Mighty pretty. And ain't it red?'

Proxy

by Talmage Powell

When I left her apartment, I skedaddled straight to. Mr. Friedland's estate. I left the car standing in the driveway and went in the big stone mansion like a coon with a pack on his trail.

I asked the butler where Mr. Friedland was, and the butler said our boss was in the study. So I busted in the study and closed the heavy walnut door behind me quick.

Mr. Friedland was at his desk. He looked up, bugged for a second by me coming in this way. But he didn't bless me out. He got up quick and said, 'What's the matter, William?'

I knuckled some sweat off my forehead, walked to the desk, and laid the envelope down. The envelope had a thousand smackers, cash, in it.

Mr. Friedland picked up the money. He looked a little addlepated.

'You did go to Marla Scanlon's apartment, William?'

'Yes, sir.'

'She was there?'

'Yes, sir.'

'But she didn't accept the money? William, I simply can't believe it.'

I couldn't think of an easy way to explain it to him. 'She's dead, Mr. Friedland.'

He cut his keen eyes from the money to me. He was a lean, handsome man who looked about thirty-five years old in the face. It was just the pure white hair that hinted at his real age.

'Dead?' he said. 'How, William?'

'Looked to me like somebody strangled her to death. I didn't hang around to make sure. There's bruises on her neck, and her tongue is stuck out and all swelled up like a hunk of bleached liver. She was a mighty fetching hunk of female,' I added with a sigh.

'Yes,' Mr. Friedland said, 'she was.'

'But she don't look so good now.'

'Was she alone in the apartment?'

'I reckon. I didn't feel the urge to poke around. Just had a look at her there on her living-room floor and hightailed it here.'

Mr. Friedland absently put the thousand bucks in his inside coat pocket. 'She was alive three hours ago. She phoned me, just before I went out. I returned, gave you the envelope, and you went to her place and found her dead. Three hours. She was killed between two and five this afternoon.'

'Could have been a lot of traffic in that much time, Mr. Friedland.'

'I doubt it. Not today. Today she was expecting a caller with a white envelope. William, you didn't see anyone on your way out of the building?'

'No, sir.'

'Phone anyone? Speak to anyone?'

'Not a soul, Mr. Friedland, until I got here and asked the butler where you was.'

'Good. You're always a good man, William.'

'Yes, sir,' I said. 'I try to be.' Which was no lie. I'm a hillbilly from near Comfort, North Carolina, which is back up in the mountains. It's a mighty poor place, believe me. Mr. Friedland came up there one summer for a week of fishing. I worked for him that week, and when the week was over he said as how would I like to keep working for him. He said I was intelligent and clean-cut and had respect for other people. He said he needed a chauffeur and a man to do errands and personal chores. He said I would have quarters on a nice estate and steady pay. So naturally I jumped at the chance. That was near five years ago, and I'm glad to say that Mr. Friedland has come to depend on me as few folks can depend on a personal worker. He trusts me and knows I can keep my mouth shut. And that means a lot to a bigshot newspaper publisher and television station owner like Mr. Friedland.

While I was simmering down and losing the shakes from my experience in Miss Marla Scanlon's apartment, Mr. Friedland was busy on the phone. He called Judge Harrison Corday and Mr. Robert Grenick, who is the prosecuting attorney. They were both close friends of Mr. Friedland. He told them to drop everything, he had to see them right away. He said a thing of utmost importance had happened which couldn't be talked about on the phone. He asked them to come to his study pronto, which they did.

Judge Corday got there first. He was one of the youngest superior court judges in the state. He liked parties and booze, and it was beginning to show around the softening edges of his face. He was a big, reddish man. He'd been a famous football star in college.

He said to Mr. Friedland, 'What's up, Arch? I've got a dinner engagement and...'

'You may not want any dinner when you hear what I have to say,' Mr. Friedland said. 'To save a lot of repetitions, we'll wait until Bob Grenick arrives.'

Judge Corday didn't press Mr. Friedland, knowing it would do no good. He sat down and lighted a dollar cigar and tried to read Mr. Friedland's lean, tight face.

Mr. Grenick showed up almost before Judge Corday got his cigar going good. Bald, chubby, and middle-aged, Mr. Grenick had thick, heavy lips and thick, heavy eyes. Both his lips and eyes always looked slightly damp, like a lizard's back that lives in a spring branch.

As soon as Mr. Grenick was in the study and the door safely closed, Mr. Friedland said, 'Tell them, William, what you just told me.'

'Miss Marla Scanlon is dead,' I said.

The judge took it without blinking an eye. The state's attorney, Mr. Grenick, choked, put a hand to his neck, fumbled for a chair, and sat down.

'How?' Judge Corday said, cool.

'Murdered, I reckon,' I said.

Mr. Grenick made noises like he was having a hard time getting air.

'By what means?' the judge asked.

'Choked to death, it looked like,' I said.

'When?'

'Sometime between two and five,' Mr. Friedland put in.

'What makes you think I have any interest until the murderer is caught and I act in official capacity?' Mr. Grenick said raggedly. 'I hardly knew Marla Scanlon.'

'Oh, come off it, Bob,' Mr. Friedland said. 'Marla Scanlon worked artfully and most skillfully. One by one she compromised the three of us. She didn't stretch her luck. We three were enough. She had her gold mine. She was content. She didn't intend to incur further risk by developing, in a manner of speaking, a source of silver.'

Mr. Grenick got half out of his chair, gripping its arms. 'I deny any . . .'

'Please shut up,' Mr. Friedland said quietly. 'None of us is on trial, not yet. But we're the three who might have killed her. It's reasonably certain that one of us did. She's milked you the longest, Harrison. I was next. Bob, you're her third and final golden goose. Between us, we've contributed, over a period of time, something like a total of sixty thousand dollars.'

'Too bad we never reported all that stashed cash to the income tax people,' Judge Corday said. 'They might have taken her off our backs.'

'And the hides from our backs right along with her,' Mr. Friedland said.

'How'd you find out all this?' Mr. Grenick asked. 'About me, I mean?'

'That's a rather silly question, Bob,' Mr. Friedland said. 'I'm still a top reporter when it comes to digging out the facts. And I have the resources of a metropolitan newspaper at my disposal, don't forget.'

'All right,' Judge Corday said, like he was on the bench considering a motion by a lawyer. 'It's laid out between us. We three were her patsys. Each had the same reason to dispose of her. We're cruising, in a word, in the same leaky boat. Now it remains to determine whether or not we have a paddle. Unfortunately, I have no alibi for the three hours between two and five this afternoon. Have you, Bob?'

'What?' Mr. Grenick was looking sort of gray, like a prospect for a dose of calomel.

'Where were you between two and five this afternoon?'

'I was . . .'

'Yes, Bob?' Mr. Friedland prompted.

Mr. Grenick lifted his eyes and looked at his friends. 'I didn't go in, understand. A block away, I turned the car. I didn't go all the way to her apartment.'

'You were going to see Marla?' the judge asked.

'Yes. I was going to appeal to her, to prove to her that I couldn't afford the blackmail tariff any longer. I was going to convince her that she'd have to be satisfied with less – or nothing at all. I simply couldn't rake up the money. I'm not as well heeled as you two.'

'But you got cold feet,' Mr. Friedland said. 'You didn't actually see her?'

'That's right, Arch, and you've got to believe me.'

'Whether or not we believe you,' the judge said, 'cuts little ice. The important thing is that you have no alibi. How about you, Arch?'

Mr. Friedland shook his head. 'I got a call from her at two o'clock. She reminded me that William was due at five with a thousand dollars. I drove out for a quiet, private look at some acreage I may purchase. I came back in time to send William on his errand.'

'So any one of us might have killed her,' the judge said.

'Listen,' Mr. Grenick said in a tight voice. 'I didn't do it. But if a scandal of this sort brushed off on me, I'm ruined. The three of us,' his eyes looked wetter than usual, 'are ruined. There are too many people in city hall and police headquarters who'd like to collect our scalps. We can't hush up a thing as big as murder, not even if Arch does control the press and TV.'

'Precisely,' Mr. Friedland said. 'Sometimes, Bob, you almost convince me you have a mind, in addition to the cunning you've shown in the political jungles. We cannot cover this thing.'

'So what do you propose?' Judge Corday asked.

'An unbreakable gentleman's agreement,' Mr. Friedland said. 'Whichever of the three of us is nailed, he must bear the entire thing alone. He must not turn to his friends for help or implicate them in the slightest. He must stand firm on the statement that he, and only he, was involved with Marla Scanlon. Whichever of us is doomed will at least have the satisfaction of knowing that he shielded his friends.'

'It might be rough,' the judge said. 'When a man's slapped in the face with murder, the natural reaction is to name others, to confuse the issue, to point suspicion elsewhere.'

'I know,' Mr. Friedland nodded, 'and that's my reason for calling you here. We must decide in advance. We must agree that the two who escape will, throughout the future, stand by the loser's loved ones in any crisis, any trouble, as if the loser himself were still there.'

'Mr. Friedland,' I said.

He turned his head in my direction. 'Yes, William?'

'All the time you been talking,' I said, 'I been thinking. I got an idear.'

'William,' Mr. Grenick said in a sore tone, 'we've far more important things to consider than any ideas you...'

Mr. Friedland shut him up with a motion of his hand. 'I don't think we have anything to lose by listening to you,' Mr. Friedland said. 'Go ahead, William.'

'Thank you, sir. You see, Mr. Friedland, you've been real nice to me, giving me a chance to live like I never knowed people live, when I was a hillbilly back up beyond Comfort, North Carolina.'

Mr. Grenick groaned. 'This is no time for asinine, emotional speeches.'

'Yes, sir,' I said. 'Anyhow, I'm all through speechifying. I just wanted Mr. Friedland to know one of the reasons I'd be willing to do you-all the favor of standing trial for Miss Marla Scanlon's murder.'

I had their attention now, believe me. Right then, you could have heard a mouse crossing the attic, only of course there wasn't none in Mr. Friedland's attic.

'William,' Mr. Friedland said finally, 'I'm touched. But I suspect that you haven't quite finished.'

'No sir, Mr. Friedland. Not quite. All three of you have society wives and fine kids and fancy homes and just everything to make life good. You stand to lose a real passel. But me, I got nobody but myself. And I never before had a chance to get me a stake together.'

'How much?' Judge Corday asked.

'Well, you been paying Miss Marla Scanlon plenty. One final payment – to me – will finish it for good. Just chip in five thousand dollars apiece, and I'll protect you all from the aftermath of this terrible thing.'

'I won't do it,' Mr. Grenick said, 'not five thou – '

'Yes, Bob, I think you will,' Mr. Friedland said. He eased his backside to the edge of his desk and brought his eyes back to me. 'How do you propose to do it, William?'

'It ought to be simple as picking corn when the sun ain't hot,' I said, 'With your newspapers and TV on my side, and Judge Corday on the bench, and Mr. Grenick handling the case of the state, I ought to come off all right. I'll say that I had been hanky-pank with Marla Scanlon. I'll say she was giving me the boot. I'll say we got in a big fight and I lost my head and killed her without really meaning to. Nobody in this town really cares that she's gone, nobody to question or suspect what you do. I figure the judge should give me about three years for manslaughter. I'll behave good and be on parole inside of a year.'

'And then?' Judge Corday said.

'I'll just take my fifteen thousand and go back to Comfort,' I said. 'None of us has got to worry about any of the others going back on the contract, account of we're all in this together and we sink or swim together.'

'William,' Mr. Friedland said, 'I think you've got a deal. How about it, friends?'

Both the judge and Mr. Grenick were quick to nod.

'I suggest,' the judge said, 'that you and William contrive to rehearse a bit in private, Bob.'

'A good idea,' the prosecutor said.

'And you've fine material to work with here,' Mr. Friedland said. 'You won't have to worry about William botching his part.'

'Well, gentlemen,' I said, 'let's get finished up here with the practice questions and all, soon's we can. I reckon I ought to get to police headquarters in a reasonable time. It'll look better if I surrender myself and show them how sorry I am for what I done to that girl.'

'Excellent, William, excellent, 'Mr. Friedland said.

I got to admit it looked pretty excellent to me too. I'd go back to Comfort a little over a year from now with over fifty thousand dollars, counting the fifteen thousand these men would cough up.

Miss Marla Scanlon, in life, had had an eye on the future.

When I'd made her open the wall safe in her apartment before I strangled her I'd picked up a little over forty thousand.

Folks around Comfort, North Carolina, are all eligible for this poverty program the government is running. It'll sure be nice, going back and being the richest man in the whole durn town. The air is clean, the scenery eye-popping, the likker mellow, and the girls all corn-fed beauties. I might even hire myself a chauffeur and a personal errand boy – only I'll make sure his name ain't William.

The Intangible Threat

by Joseph Payne Brennan

Late one gray and overcast afternoon some years ago, I was visiting my investigator friend, Lucius Leffing, at seven Autumn Street. Conversation had faltered and presently we sat in silence as a cold November wind rattled the windows.

Leffing remained hunched in his favorite chair, an expression of brooding melancholy on his face. There were times when the tedium of mere existence weighed on him heavily. On such occasions he would lapse into silence and unsociability. Though I had learned to endure my friend's black moods, I dreaded them.

With rare exceptions, only two events could scatter the gloom: the promise of an interesting case, or the discovery and acquisition of some treasured bit of Victoriana – a Carder's bowl, a prized paperweight, or even a photograph taken before the turn of the century.

But Leffing's finances had not permitted any recent purchases from the local antique shops, and there had been no case of consequence to engage his attention.

I was about to leave when the doorbell rang. Leffing arose with a listless air and crossed to the entrance hall. I heard an earnest feminine voice; a moment later my friend ushered in an attractive young woman whom he introduced as Miss Eunice Armiston.

Miss Armiston, whom I judged to be in her mid twenties, had the type of face which used to be described as 'a sweet oval'; it was flawlessly symmetrical and delicate, but marred by a deep frown of worry or apprehension.

When we were seated, she spread her coat across the back of her chair and leaned forward.

'Recently, a friend of mine, Mrs. Julia Newington, mentioned that you had helped her some years ago when a family problem arose which threatened to explode into scandal. She had the highest praise for your discretion and for your dispatch in resolving the difficulty.'

Leffing nodded. 'I recall the case quite well. The problem required rather delicate handling but I was fortunate enough to settle matters.' He glanced at me. 'You will not remember the case, Brennan; it took place before your advent.' He then turned back towards our lovely visitor. 'And now you have a problem, Miss Armiston?'

'I am worried about my aunt,' she said. 'I did not go to the police because I dread publicity, and also because there is so little really tangible to report. Under the circumstances, you were the first person who came to mind.'

'What is the problem then?'

'I am convinced that my aunt's life is in danger!'

Leffing's angular face assumed an expression of interest and expectancy. 'From what source, Miss Armiston?'

Our client hesitated briefly and then plunged ahead. 'From my cousin, that is, from my aunt's adopted child, Ronald Bladell. He is actually no relation to me at all. He was the illegitimate son of my aunt's maid. When the maid unexpectedly died, leaving the infant, my aunt felt sorry for him and took out adoption papers. He was always a problem child. Now that he is grown, he preys on my aunt for money. She is quite wealthy, you know – Mrs. Frederick Bladell. Her husband died when he was young, but he left her the Bladell mining properties.'

'Leffing nodded. 'I have heard of the Bladell holdings. Continue, Miss Armiston. What were the exact circumstances which brought you here? Ronald Bladell threatened your aunt?'

Eunice Armiston's frown deepened. 'Well, not *directly*. They had a serious quarrel after lunch, but they patched it up and afterwards Ronald was as sweet as honey. That's what worries me, it's so out of character! And then, as he was leaving the house afterwards, I heard him mumbling to himself as he came down the porch steps. I was in the garden but he didn't see me. I couldn't hear what he said very clearly but one phrase did come through. He muttered, "I'll fix the old witch"! It made my blood run cold. And there was a look of pure hatred, pure evil, on his face as he said it. I am positive he means to harm my aunt!'

'He would benefit by her death?' Leffing inquired.

'Yes, my aunt has remembered him in her will – generously.'

Leffing sat without speaking for a few minutes. 'While I have great respect for feminine intuition, Miss Armiston,' he said finally, 'you must realize that we can scarcely take any action merely because of a muttered comment addressed to no one. Perhaps he mumbled, "I'd like to fix the old witch!" Angry people often mumble threats which are afterwards forgotten. If all of them were successfully prosecuted for making menacing remarks, our jails would not hold them. Can you give us any details of the quarrel? Can you recall specifically what was said?'

Miss Armiston flushed. 'I wasn't in the room. I suppose I, well, eavesdropped a bit. My aunt had just recently returned from a Florida vacation. When she refused to give Ronald money over and above his regular allowance – he is twenty-three, Mr. Leffing – he became abusive. He said she had no right to be down in Florida spending money while he was "slaving away". Actually, he has an undemanding job as assistant gardener to the local Botanical Experiment Bureau. The hours are short and the work is light, but he doesn't earn enough for liquor, women and gambling. And my aunt's allowance – generous under the circumstances – even when added to his pay, isn't enough to meet his extravagances either. He accused my aunt of being miserly and selfish. Finally, when he saw that insults had no effect, he apologized and became very contrite. He overdid it so, it was sickening. My aunt must have known it was all a pose, but she was very fond of him at one time and she permitted him to make up.'

She paused, biting her lip. 'After the argument, he couldn't do enough. He cleaned up some chores which have been neglected because both cook and the yard man have been ill. He carried out trash, burned leaves, ground up a supply of fresh coffee and so on. Well, afterwards, my aunt softened a little in spite of herself. But she didn't give him any money. That was when he left the house muttering that threat, and with that horrible, gloating, venomous look on his face!'

'Possibly,' I suggested, 'he was gloating because he had managed to gloss over the argument so deftly.'

Eunice Armiston shook her head. 'No, it wasn't that. I know him too well. I am certain he is planning something malicious, something deadly!'

Leffing frowned. 'Did he at any time during the argument hint at anything he might do – in the nature of revenge?'

'No, he didn't.'

'And you can think of no specific circumstance or incident which gives solid ground to your apprehension?'

Miss Armiston looked miserable. 'Just the argument and that mumbled threat!'

'I fear we have no case, Miss Armiston. As I said before, if people were arrested for muttering threats to themselves, most of us would be imprisoned at one time or another.'

'Well, I *hate* him,' she burst out passionately. 'The little sneak thief! He's capable of anything! Even murder!'

Anger enhanced Eunice Armiston's attractiveness. Her flushed face, flashing eyes and aura of scornful animation fascinated me.

But all this was lost on Leffing. He pondered her words in his usual clinical fashion. 'You use the term "sneak thief," Miss Armiston. Is your aunt's adopted son a thief?'

'We have no proof, but in my opinion he is. A number of items have turned up missing after one of his visits. Today after he left, my aunt missed a necklace which she had brought back from Florida. It was on a table in the room where the argument took place. My aunt shrugged it off, pretending that it was probably mislaid and will turn up later, but I think she knows that Ronald took it. I've always felt, Mr. Leffing,' she added, 'that a thief is capable of anything!'

Leffing nodded. 'You may be right, Miss Armiston. Was the necklace of much value?'

Our client shook her head. 'Oh, no. It was just one of those colorful seed necklaces they make and sell in the south. Its value is negligible. But my aunt was annoyed. I believe she bought the necklace as a present for a little girl who lives next door.'

Leffing placed his fingertips together. 'Why would Ronald Bladell steal a seed necklace? Surely he must have known it was virtually valueless.'

Miss Armiston shrugged. 'I suppose it was just an impulse. Light-fingered people will pick up anything. I understand. It becomes a habit with them.'

Leffing frowned. 'Miss Armiston, can you describe the necklace in any detail?'

She looked at him in surprise. 'Well, since I attached little importance to it, I did not observe it in much detail. But let me see. The beads, or seeds I suppose I should say, were bright red and shiny with black at one end, a sort of tiny black cap. Actually, strung together, they were quite eye-catching.'

Abruptly, Leffing arose from his chair. 'At what time does your aunt have dinner?'

She gazed up at him in mounting confusion. 'At quarter to six. But why do you ask, Mr. Leffing?'

He ignored the question. 'You must telephone your aunt at once and insist that dinner be delayed until you have returned. We will accompany you.'

Miss Armiston glanced at her watch. 'It is too late to telephone now. It is already after five. But why –'

Leffing seemed unaccountably agitated. 'Too late, you say? "After five"? Please explain yourself, Miss Armiston! Isn't that unusual?'

Eunice Armiston blushed again. 'My aunt is – a bit eccentric, I'm afraid. From five until seven the telephone bell is disconnected. My aunt will not be disturbed by telephone calls either just before or after her dinner. It is a great inconvenience to her friends, but she will not change her habits.'

Leffing stared at her. 'Great heavens!' Then, swiftly, he turned to me. 'Brennan, you drove here?'

I nodded.

He started toward the door. 'Quickly, then! There is not a moment to lose! Miss Armiston will give us her aunt's address!'

Three minutes later we were in the tangle of five o'clock traffic. When Miss Armiston revealed that her aunt lived in Bethany Woods, I realized every minute would count.

As seems inevitable under urgent circumstances, traffic lights, slow-moving trucks and tortoise-like drivers conspired against us. Leffing remained silent for some time, but as I glanced at his rigid face, I knew he was all but bursting with frantic impatience.

As we approached our fourth red light, he looked quickly along both both ways of the intersecting street. 'Go through it, Brennan!' he instructed. 'Go through it!'

I shot through and began to make better time. I have only a kaleidoscopic memory of that drive. I know that I went through several more red lights and that as I neared the end of Whalley Avenue, approaching Woodbridge, I saw the flashing lights of a police car in my rear-view mirror. I pressed the accelerator almost to the floor.

The speedometer hit seventy, but the police car gained. Slowing for the curves, I held at about sixty.

The police car shot alongside as we neared Bethany. I considered making one final break but thought better of it and pulled over.

By the time the police driver got out of his car, Leffing was already holding out identification which certified that he was legally authorized to act in the capacity of private detective. He spoke rapidly as the office examined the card.

Suddenly the police driver nodded, hurried back to his car and roared away ahead of us, siren wailing, lights flashing.

Our escort knew the location of the Bladell property. We pulled up behind him in front of a stately Georgian mansion, screened by blue spruce and cedars.

We ran up a curving flagstone path to the porticoed porch. Leffing pressed the bell but Miss Armiston shook her head and fumbled in her handbag. 'Disconnected,' she explained. 'Five to seven.'

A moment later she found the key and led us into an entrance hall.

'The dining room?' Leffing inquired.

'Straight ahead,' Eunice Armiston told him.

He literally ran past us. We arrived in the dining room just in time to witness a bizarre incident.

A grey-haired matriarch, majestic in her outraged dignity, had risen from her seat at the table, a coffee cup still lifted in one hand.

'What is the explanation of this intrusion?' she demanded.

In response, Leffing literally leaped across the room and knocked the coffee cup from her hand. The cup crashed to the floor, splattering coffee in every direction.

Mrs. Bladell stared at the shattered cup. Then she lifted her eyes and caught sight of the police car driver. 'Officer, arrest this maniac!'

Leffing bowed courteously. 'My sincere apologies, Mrs. Bladell. But had you drunk that cup of coffee, it might have been your last. A chemical analysis, I believe, will reveal abrin, one of the deadliest poisons known!'

Mrs. Bladell looked down at the spilled coffee seeping into the rug.

'Abrin? How did it get into my coffee, then? And who are you?'

Leffing introduced himself. 'Did you ever find your missing necklace, Mrs. Bladell?'

She shook her head. 'No. But what on earth?'

'Just this, Mrs. Bladell,' Leffing explained, 'the necklace, as it was described to me by your niece, consisted of jequirity peas strung together. The jequirity was introduced into Florida where the seeds are used to make bead jewelry of various kinds. The jequirity, or crabs-eye pea, is pretty and colorful, but unfortunately these bright seeds contain abrin, a toxic poison. A single seed contains enough poison to kill an adult.'

We all stood staring in astonishment as he continued.

'I fear, Mrs. Bladell,' he went on, 'that your adopted son, probably as a result of his work at the local Botanical Experiment Bureau, was aware of the toxic content of jequirity seeds. Your niece indicated that Ronald may have stolen the necklace. I did not immediately fathom the implications of this until I suddenly recalled that Miss Armiston had also mentioned that Ronald had ground up fresh coffee for you early this afternoon. I am convinced the missing necklace, sans string and clasp, disappeared into the coffee grinder, Mrs. Bladell!'

A subsequent analysis of the remaining ground coffee confirmed Leffing's belief. The coffee contained enough abrin to kill twenty people.

As Leffing and I sat discussing the case some nights later,

between sips of my friend's choice cognac, I sighed and shook my head. 'Your powers continue to confound me,' I admitted, 'but *must* you be so melodramatic, Leffing?'

'Melodramatic, Brennan? How so?'

'Well, hang it all, did you *have* to dash that cup out of the old lady's hand? Couldn't you have, well, just told her not to drink it?'

Leffing glanced around his Victorian gaslit living room with an air of deep contentment. 'My dear Brennan,' he replied, settling back in his beloved chair, 'One can never take chances with a strong-willed old lady. Had I not dashed the cup from her hand, Mrs. Bladell, in spite of my warning, perhaps *because* of it, might have perversely swallowed the coffee on the spot! I have known these things to happen.'

I was not convinced. Leffing's tendency to dramatize situations is one of his incurable faults. But I said no more. When one is drinking a friend's twenty-year-old, cask-mellowed cognac, one must not dwell unduly on his foibles.

The Cost of Kent Castwell

by Avram Davidson

Clem Goodhue met the train with his taxi. If old Mrs. Merriman were aboard he would be sure of at least one passenger. Furthermore, old Mrs. Merriman had somehow gotten the idea that the minimum fare was a dollar. It was really seventy-five cents, but Clem had never been able to see a reason for telling her that. However, she was not aboard that morning. Sam Wells was. He was coming back from the city – been to put in a claim to have his pension increased – but Sam Wells wouldn't pay five cents to ride any distance under five miles. Clem disregarded him.

After old Sam a thin, brown-haired kid got off the train. Next came a girl, also thin and also brown-haired, who Clem thought was maybe the kid's teenage sister. Actually, it was the kid's mother.

After *that* came Kent Castwell.

Clem had seen him before, early in the summer. Strangers were not numerous in Ashby, particularly strangers who got ugly and caused commotions in bars. So Clem wouldn't forget him in a hurry. Big, husky fellow. Always seemed to be sneering at something. But the girl and the kid hadn't been with him then.

'Taxi?' Clem called.

Castwell ignored him, began to take down luggage from the train. But the young girl holding the kid by the hand turned and said, 'Yes – just a minute.'

'Where to?' Clem asked, when the luggage was in the taxi.

'The old Peabody place,' the girl said. 'You know where that is?'

'Yes. But nobody lives there any more.'

'Somebody does now. Us.' The big man swore as he fiddled with the handle of the right-hand door. It was tied with ropes. 'Why don't you fix this thing or get a new one?'

'Costs money,' Clem said. Then, 'Peabody place? Have to charge you three dollars for that.'

'Let's go dammit, let's go!'

After they'd started off, Castwell said, 'I'm giving you two bucks. Probably twice what it's worth, anyway.'

Half-turning his head, Clem protested. 'I told you, mister, it was three.'

'And I'm telling you, mister,' Castwell mimicked the driver's New England accent, 'that I'm giving you two.'

Clem argued that the Peabody place was far out. He mentioned the price of gas, the bad condition of the road, the wear on the tires. The big man yawned. Then he used a word which Clem rarely used himself, and never in the presence of women and children. But this young woman and child didn't seem to notice.

'Stop off at Nickerson's Real Estate Office,' Castwell said.

Levi P. Nickerson, who was also the County Tax Assessor, said, 'Mr. Castwell. I assume this is Mr. Castwell?'

'If that's your assumption, go right ahead,' said Kent. And laughed.

It wasn't a pleasant laugh. The woman smiled faintly, so L.P. Nickerson allowed himself an economical chuckle. Then he cleared his throat. City people had odd ideas of what was funny. Meanwhile, though –

'Now, Mr. Castwell. About this place you're renting. I didn't realize – you didn't mention – that you had this little one, here.'

Kent said, 'What if I didn't mention it? It's my own business. I haven't got all *day* –'

Nickerson pointed out that the Peabody place stood all alone, isolated, with no other house for at least a mile and no other children in the neighborhood. Mrs. Castwell – if, indeed, she *was* – said that this wouldn't matter much, because Kathie would be in school most of the day.

'School. Well, that's it, you see. The school bus, in the first place, will have to go three miles off what's been its regular route to pick up your little girl. And that means the road will have to be plowed regular – snow gets real deep in these parts, you know. Up till now, with nobody living in the old Peabody place, we never had to bother with the road. Now, this means,' and he began to count off on his fingers, 'first, it'll cost Ed Westlake, he drives the school bus, more than he figured on when he bid for the contract; second, it'll cost the County to keep your road open. That's besides the cost of the girl's schooling, which is third.'

Kent Castwell said that was tough, wasn't it?' 'Let's have the keys, Nick,' he said.

A flicker of distaste at the familiarity crossed the real estate man's face. 'You don't seem to realize that all this extra expense to the County isn't covered by the tax assessment on the Peabody place,' he pointed out. 'Now, it just so happens that there's a house right on the outskirts of town become available this week. Miss Sarah Beech passed on, and her sister, Miss Lavinia, moved in with their married sister, Mrs. Calvin Adams. 'Twon't cost *you* any more, and it would save *us* considerable.'

Castwell, sneering, got up. 'What! Me live where some old-maid landlady can be on my neck all the time about messing up her pretty things? Thanks a lot. No thanks.' He held out his hand. 'The keys, kid. Gimme the keys.'

Mr. Nickerson gave him the keys. Afterwards he was to say, and to say often, that he wished he'd thrown them into Lake Amastanquit, instead.

The income of the Castwell menage was not large and consisted of a monthly check and a monthly money order. The check came on the fifteenth, from a city trust company, and was assumed by some to be inherited income. Others argued in favor of its being a remittance paid by Castwell's family to keep him away. The money order was made out to Louise Cane, and signed by an army sergeant in Alaska. The young woman said this was alimony, and that Sergeant Burndall was her former husband. Tom Tally, at the grocery store, had her sign the endorsement twice, as Louise Cane and as Louise Castwell. Tom was a cautious man.

Castwell gave Louise a hard time, there was no doubt about that. If she so much as walked in between the sofa, on which he spent most of his time, and the television, he'd leap up and belt her. More than once both she and the kid had to run out of the house to get away from him. He wouldn't follow, as a rule, because he was barefooted, as a rule, and it was too much trouble to put his shoes on.

Lie on the sofa and drink beer and watch television all afternoon, and hitch into town and drink bar whiskey and watch television all evening – that was Kent Castwell's daily schedule. He got to know who drove along the road regularly, at what time, and in which direction, and he'd be there, waiting. There was more than one who could have dispensed with the pleasure of his company, but he'd get out in the road and wave his arms and not move until the car he got in front of stopped.

What could you do about it? Put him in jail?

Sure you could.

He hadn't been living there a week before he got into a fight at the Ashby Bar.

'Disturbing the peace, using profane and abusive language, and resisting arrest – that will be ten dollars or ten days on each of the charges,' said Judge Paltiel Bradford. 'And count yourself lucky it's not more. Pay the Clerk.'

But Castwell, his ugly leer in no way improved by the dirt and bruises on his face, said, 'I'll take jail.'

Judge Bradford's long jaw set, then loosened. 'Look here, Mr. Castwell, that was just legal language on my part. The jail is closed up. Hasn't been anybody in there since July.' It was then November. 'It would have to be heated, and illuminated, and the water turned on, and a guard hired. To say nothing of feeding you. Now, I don't see why the County should be put to all that expense on your account. You pay the Clerk thirty dollars. You haven't got it on you, take till tomorrow. Well?'

'I'll take the jail.'

'It's most inconvenient –'

'That's too bad, Your Honor.'

The judge glared at him. Gamaliel Coolidge, the District Attorney, stood up. 'Perhaps the court would care to suspend sentence,' he suggested. 'Seeing it is the defendant's first offense.'

The Court did care. But the next week Kent was back again, on the same charge. Altogether the sentence now came to sixty dollars, or sixty days. And again Castwell chose jail.

'I don't generally do this,' the judge said, fuming. 'But I'll let you pay your fine off in installments. Considering you have a wife and child.'

'Uh-uh. I'll take jail.'

'You won't like the food!' warned His Honor.

Castwell said he guessed the food would be up to the legal requirements. If it wasn't, he said, the State Board of Prison Inspectors would hear about it.

Some pains were taken to see that the food served Kent during his stay in jail was beyond the legal requirement – if not much beyond. The last time the State Board has inspected the County Jail it had cost the tax-payers two hundred dollars in repairs. It was costing them quite enough to incarcerate Kent Castwell, as it was, although the judge had reduced the cost by ordering the sentences to run concurrently.

All in all, Kent spent over a month in jail that winter, at various times. It seemed to some that whenever his money ran out he let the County support him, and let the woman and child fend for themselves. Tom Talley gave them a little credit at the store. Not much.

Ed Westlake, when he bid again for the school bus contract, added the cost of going three miles out of his way to pick up Kathie. The County had no choice but to meet the extra charge. It was considered very thoughtless of Louise to wait till *after* the contract was signed before leaving Castwell and going back to the city with her child. The side road to the Peabody place didn't have to be plowed so often, but it still had to be plowed *some*. That extra cost, just for one man! It was maddening.

It almost seemed – no, it *did* seem – as if Kent Castwell was deliberately setting himself in the face of New England respectability and thrift. The sacred words, 'Eat it up, wear it out, make it do, or do without,' didn't mean a thing to him. He wasn't just indifferent. He was hostile.

Ashby was not a thriving place. It had no industries. It was not a resort town, being far from sea and mountains alike, with only the shallow, muddy waters of Lake Amastanquit for a pleasure spot. Its thin-soiled farms and meager woodlots produced a scanty return for the hard labor exacted. The young people continued to leave. Kent Castwell, unfortunately, showed no signs of leaving.

All things considered, it was not surprising that Ashby had no artists' colony. It *was* rather surprising, then, that Clem Goodhue, meeting the train with his taxi, recognized Bob Laurel at once as an artist. When asked afterwards how he had known, Clem looked smug, and said that he had once been to Provincetown.

The conversation, as Clem recalled it afterwards, began with Bob Laurel's asking where he could find a house which offered low rent, peace and quiet, and a place to paint.

'So I recommended Kent Castwell,' Clem said. He was talking to Sheriff Erastus Nickerson (Levi P.'s cousin) at the time.

'"Peace and *quiet?*"' the sheriff repeated. 'I know Laurel's a city fellow, and an artist, but still and all –'

They were seated in the bar of the Ashby House, drinking their weekly small glass of beer. 'I looked at it this way, Erastus,' the taxi-man said. 'Sure, there's empty houses all around that he could rent. Suppose *he* – this artist fellow – suppose *he* picks one off on the side road with nobody else living in it? Suppose *he* comes up with a wife out of somewhere, and suppose *she* has a school-age child?'

'You're right, Clem.'

'"Course I'm right. Bad enough for the County to be put to all that cost for *one* house, let alone two.'

'You're right, Clem. But will he stay with Castwell?'

Clem shrugged. 'That I can't say. But I did my best.'

Laurel stayed with Castwell. He really had no choice. The big man agreed to take him in as lodger and to give over the front room for a studio. And, holding out offers of insulating the house, putting in another window, and who knows what else, Kent Castwell persuaded the unwary artist to pay several months' rent in advance. Needless to say, he drank up the money and did nothing at all in the way of the promised improvements.

Neither District Attorney Gamaliel Coolidge nor Sheriff Nickerson, nor for that matter, anyone else, showed Laurel much sympathy. He had grounds for a civil suit, they said;

nothing else. It should be a lesson to him not to throw his money around in the future, they said.

So the unhappy artist stayed on at the old Peabody place, buying his own food and cutting his own wood, and painting, painting, painting. And all the time he knew full well that his leering landlord only waited for him to go into town in order to help himself to both food and wood.

Laurel invited Clem to have a glass of beer with him more than once, just to have someone to tell his troubles to. Besides stealing his food and fuel, Kent Castwell, it seemed, played the TV at full blast when Laurel wanted to sleep; if it was too late for TV, he set the radio to roaring. At moments when the artist was intent on delicate brush-work, Castwell would decide to bring in stove-wood and drop it on the floor so that the whole house shook.

'He talks to himself in that loud, rough voice of his,' Bob Laurel complained. 'He has a filthy mouth. He makes fun of my painting. He –'

'I tell you what it is,' Clem said. 'Kent Castwell has no consideration for others. That's what it is. Yep.'

Bets were taken in town, of a ten-cent cigar per bet, on how long Laurel would stand for it. Levi Nickerson, the County Tax Assessor, thought he'd leave as soon as his rent was up. Clem's opinion was that he'd leave soon. 'Money don't mean much to city people,' he pointed out.

Clem won.

When he came into Nickerson's house, Levi, who was sitting close to the small fire in the kitchen stove, wordlessly handed over the cigar. Clem nodded, put it in is pocket. Mrs. Abby Nickerson sat next to her husband, wearing a man's sweater. It had belonged to her late father, whose heart had failed to survive the first re-election of Franklin D. Roosevelt, and it still had a lot of wear left in it. Abby was unraveling old socks, and winding the wool into a ball. 'Waste not, want not,' was her motto – as well as that of every other old-time local resident.

On the stove a kettle steamed thinly. Two piles of used envelopes were on the table. They had all been addressed to the Tax Assessor's office of the County, and had been carefully opened so as not to mutilate them. While Clem watched, Levi Nickerson removed one of the envelopes from its place on top of the uncovered kettle. The mucilage on its flaps loosened by steam, it opened out easily to Nickerson's touch. He proceeded to refold it and then reseal it so that the used outside was now inside; then he added it to the other pile.

Saved the County eleven dollars this way last year,' he observed. 'Shouldn't wonder but what I don't make it twelve this year, maybe twelve-fifty.' Clem gave a small appreciative grunt. 'Where is he?' the Tax Assessor asked.

'Laurel? In the Ashby Bar. He's all packed. I told him to stay put. I told them to keep an eye on him, phone me here if he made a move to leave.'

He took a sheet of paper out of his pocket and put it on the table. Levi looked at it, but made no move to pick it up. To his wife he said, 'I'm expecting Erastus and Gam Coolidge over, Mrs. Nickerson. County business. I expect you can find something to do in the front of the house while we talk.'

Mrs. Levi nodded. Even words were not wasted.

A car drove up to the house.

'That's Erastus,' said his cousin. 'Gam should be along – he *is* along. Might've known he wouldn't waste gasoline; came with Erastus.'

The two men came into the kitchen. Mrs. Abby Nickerson arose and departed.

'Hope we can get this over with before nightfall,' the sheriff said. 'I don't like to drive after dark if I can help it. One of my headlights is getting dim, and they cost so darned much to replace.'

Clem cleared his throat. 'Well, here 'tis,' he said, gesturing to the paper on the table. 'Laurel's confession. "Tell the sheriff and the D.A. that I'm ready to give myself up,"' he says. '"I wrote it all down here,"' he says. Happened about two o'clock this afternoon, I guess. Straw that broke the camel's back. Kent Castwell, he was acting up as usual. Stomping and swearing out there at the Peabody place. Words were exchanged. Laurel left to go out back,' Clem said, delicately, not needing to further comment on the Peabody place's lack of indoor plumbing. 'When he come back, Castwell had taken the biggest brush he could find and smeared paint over all the pictures Laurel had been working on. Ruined them completely.'

There was a moment's silence. 'Castwell had no call to do that,' the sheriff said. 'Destroying another man's property. They tell me some of those artists get as much as a hundred dollars for a painting... What'd he do then? Laurel, I mean.'

'Picked up a piece of stovewood and hit him with it. Hit him hard.'

'No doubt about his being dead, I suppose?' the sheriff asked.

Clem shook his head. 'There was no blood or anything on the wood,' he added. 'Just another piece of stove wood... But he's dead, all right.'

After a moment Levi Nickerson said, 'His wife will have to be notified. No reason why the County should have to pay burial expenses. Hmmm. I expect she won't have any money, though. Best get in touch with those trustees who sent Castwell his money every month. *They'll* pay.'

Gamaliel Coolidge asked if anyone else knew. Clem said no. Bob Laurel hadn't told anyone else. He didn't seem to want to talk.

This time there was a longer silence.

'Do you realize how much Kent Castwell cost this County, one way or the other?' Nickerson said.

Clem said he supposed hundreds of dollars. 'Hundreds and *hundreds* of dollars,' Nickerson said.

'*And*,' the Tax Assessor went on, 'do you know what it will cost us to try this fellow – for murder in any degree or manslaughter?'

The District Attorney said it would cost thousands. 'Thousands and *thousands*... and that's just the trial,' he elaborated. 'Suppose he's found guilty and appeals? We'd be obliged to fight the appeal. More thousands. And suppose he gets a new trial? We'd have it to pay all over again.'

Levi P. Nickerson opened his mouth as though it hurt him to do so. 'What it would do to the County tax-rate...' he groaned. 'Kent Castwell,' he said, his voice becoming crips and definite, 'is not worth it. He is just not *worth* it.'

Clem took out the ten-cent cigar he'd won, sniffed it. 'My opinion,' he said, 'it would have been much better if this fellow Laurel had just packed up and left. Anybody finding Castwell's body would assume he'd fallen and hit his head. But this confession, now –'

Sheriff Erastus Nickerson said reflectively, 'I haven't read any confession. You, Gam? You, Levi? No. What you've told us, Clem, is just hearsay. Can't act on hearsay. Totally contrary to all principles of American law . . . Hmm. Mighty nice sunset.' He arose and walked over to the window. His cousin followed him. So did District Attorney Coolidge. While they were looking at the sunset Clem Goodhue, after a single glance at their backs, took the sheet of paper from the kitchen table and thrust it into the kitchen stove. There was a flare of light. It quickly died down. Clem carefully reached his hand into the stove, took out the small corner of the paper remaining, and lit his cigar with it.

The three men turned from the window.

Levi P. Nickerson was first to speak. 'Can't ask any of you to stay to supper,' he said. 'Just a few leftovers is all we're having. I expect you'll want to be going on your way.'

The two other County officials nodded.

The taxi-man said, 'I believe I'll stop by the Ashby Bar. Might be someone there wanting to catch the evening train. Night, Levi. Don't turn on the yard light for us.'

'Wasn't going to,' said Levi. 'Turning them on and off, that's what burns them out. Night, Clem, Gam, Erastus.' He closed the door after them. 'Mrs. Nickerson,' he called to his wife, 'you can come and start supper now. We finished our business.'

My Unfair Lady

by Guy Cullingford

I was sitting in a nook in the woods reading a paperback, when this little girl parted the leaves and looked in at me. At first sight she seemed no better or worse than the usual run of small females, a set of indeterminate features framed in towy pigtails which had a long way to go to reach her shoulders. She was wearing a fairly clean dress, bare legs and sandals.

'Excuse me, mister,' she said, staring at me good and hard.

'Certainly,' I said amiably. 'But the wood's big enough for both of us, and I daresay we'll get on better at a distance.'

I went on with my reading. And though I kept my eyes on the printed word, I could feel hers like a pair of gimlets boring into me.

'How about leaving me in peace?' I said. 'Be a good girl.'

She made no attempt to move. She was following her own line of thought, not mine. After a moment, she said, 'There's a gentleman being unkind to a lady under that tree.' And she turned a bit and pointed.

I felt myself getting hot under the collar, and I said, 'That's none of my business or yours either. Run away home, you nasty prying little girl. I don't want to know you.'

She stayed put, not budging an inch. For a full minute she remained silent, twisting one ankle round the other.

Then she said, 'How'd you like it if someone stuck a knife into you?'

'What!' I leapt to my feet, slamming the book shut. 'Why didn't you say that in the beginning? Where's this? What — what tree'd you say?'

She was off like a shot with me right after her. We went about twenty feet down the slope, and then the tail of the girl's little dress vanished into a tangle of undergrowth. I scrambled after her. But when we got to the foot of the tree. I stopped short, silently staring.

There the woman lay, on last year's leaves with her head supported by a beech trunk. The knife must have found the heart, for she was just as dead as the leaves, although she hadn't been there as long. There's always something pretty shocking in sudden death, and she couldn't have been more than twenty. She must have been a good-looker too. The haft of the knife was still in place, and suddenly I felt sick at my stomach. I turned away to throw up and realized with a start that the kid who brought me there had vanished; she must have melted away while I was busy taking in the situation. I hadn't time to be sick. It suddenly dawned on me that I was in a serious postion. That wretched little girl was as valuable to me as her weight in diamonds; she was my one and only alibi that I'd visited the scene of the crime and nothing more. So I had to find her again as soon as possible.

I bolted down the slope, right to the bottom where there was a kind of paddling pond crammed full of children. But though I darted here and there, and there were dozens of little girls, there wasn't a trace of the one I wanted. I tell you, I stood still, and the sweat trickled down my face. I suppose ten minutes elapsed before I gave up the search. Then I had to ask myself a question. What do I do now? I was all for racing away as fast as my legs would take me. If I'd had a hat I could have pulled down over my eyes, I don't think I should have hesitated to do that. But I was bare-headed, and I'd been behaving, in the light of later events, in what might well have been described as oddly by any interested onlooker. There were several mothers who must have spared a moment from watching Bobbie get his pants splashed on to make a mental note of my interest in little girls, perhaps were even ready to have a word with a policeman. And, by heaven, there was a policeman ready made for them, standing in the shade of the trees, no doubt presiding benignly over the frolics of the young, and all set to prevent any casualty amongst the waders.

I had a horrid vision of myself on the run – the man the police wanted to interview in connection with the murdered girl. Well, in the choice of evils it's my motto to choose the lesser. I headed for the policeman, as if in his stalwart frame lay my only hope of salvation.

'Officer,' I said in a voice that broke with uncertainty, 'Officer, I want to report a crime.'

That shook him. He was a youngish man, and he looked as if all his blood had suddenly drained into his boots. But he pulled himself together and asked me a few questions, and soon we were making it up the slope together, my heart pumping a great deal harder than was called for by the incline.

Of course, later on I got passed on to higher authority for questioning, first a detective sergeant and then an inspector, then both together. I stuck to my story, and they seemed to me to be decent fellows. They almost believed me.

What really rattled them was one of those fantastic coincidences which would be quite inadmissible in fiction. When the constable first bore me off to the police station, I was still clutching that confounded paperback, and when they took it off me, there on the cover, for them to see, was a blonde with a dagger in her heart. I hadn't even noticed the subject of the luridly painted cover until I had it pointed out to me. In the absence of any more substantial clue, blood or strands of hair or incriminating fingerprints, they had to make the most of that. In defence, I stuck to the little girl who had drawn me into my predicament; she was all I had.

'Pity you don't know her name,' commented the inspector, a shade dryly I thought.

'I don't go round asking the names of strange little girls,' I said. 'I'm not fond enough of them for that.'

The inspector nodded. 'Mind you,' he said, 'if what you're telling us is the truth, there's no need to be alarmed. If the kid's above ground we'll find her, don't you worry.'

'Then I'll not worry,' I said.

'Lucky the schools haven't broken up,' said the sergeant. 'We'll go through them with a fine-tooth comb till we find her, that is...' He paused significantly and scratched his nose. I could see he wasn't convinced.

I got to know the sergeant quite well during the next twenty-four hours – and the local schools. As far as the children were concerned, our arrival was a welcome interruption, but the teachers were less approving. Finally, at Omega Road Girls' School we struck oil.

After a short talk with the headmistress, we were shown into a classroom of the correct age group. There were about four and twenty little darlings present, with the one we were after practically indistinguishable from the rest – except to me. She was seated at a desk, second row from the front. We had been warned not to upset the little dears, so the sergeant in a voice flowing with milk and honey asked them if they'd any of them ever seen this gentleman (pointing to me) before anywhere. Up shot a forest of hands. Only one in the second row remained at desk level. You can guess whose.

'Where?' asked the sergeant.

'Pleasir, pleasir,' they changed in unison, and one being singled out by the head-mistress for a solo speech said, 'Please, Ma'am, we all saw him at the paddling pool in Hammer Wood on the afternoon the young woman got done in.'

The head-mistress shot me a frosty look, as if I should be held responsible for any psychic damage done to these innocents. At once I asked the sergeant for the privilege of half a minute's private conversation. We cowered behind the blackboard, and I whispered into his ear that the one who hadn't put up her hand was the one we were after. He emerged brushing his moustache, first one side, then the other, and said, 'I want to ask the little girl in the second row who didn't put up her hand if she has ever seen this gentleman before.'

'Speak up, Ruby Grant,' said the head-mistress, cooing at the little wretch. 'No one's going to hurt you, dear.'

The child's indeterminate features registered no expression whatever. She took her time about it, studying me with a sort of vacant earnestness.

'I never seen him in me life, Miss Birch,' she finally said. 'I don't know that gentleman at all, and –' here the lips parted in a grin to disclose a set of tiny, regular teeth ' – I don't know as I want to.'

A giggle ran round the class, and Miss Birch did nothing to suppress it. Instead, she asked mildly, 'You weren't at the pool with the others, then?'

'No, Miss Birch, Ruby wasn't at the pool with us,' said a

child who was seated behind Ruby Grant. 'She said she had to go straight home.'

'Is that right, Ruby?'

'Yes, Miss Birch. I wanted to look after me baby brother, so our mum could get a rest.'

You could practically see the halo above that flaxen crown.

'I have always found Ruby a very truthful little girl,' remarked Miss Birch, sotto voce to the sergeant.

That was that. I ask you, what could I do about it?

They had to let me go in the end, for there wasn't a shred of real evidence. They couldn't trace any connection between me and the murdered girl, and it wasn't any good bringing a prosecution on the strength of a lurid book jacket. Although I was told dozens of women volunteered to give information on my personal appearance down at the pool that afternoon. You know, the usual thing, the wild and glaring eyes, the maniacal frenzy, etcetera, etcetera. I never varied my story, however much opportunity I was given, and there was nothing known against me, and I was in steady employment.

As far as I could see, they would never nail anyone else for the wood-killing either. Like most of those girls who are found murdered, she was not known to have had any men friends. Apparently, she ran to type, quiet and reserved and self-respecting. Well, she was now, anyway, poor thing. The knife was of a common sort which might be found in the possession of any boy scout. Although it had been sharpened to a fine edge, there were no fingerprints on it. As for fallen leaves, they don't measure up to flower beds when it comes to holding the impression of a distinctive shoe heel. If I'd done the murder myself, I couldn't have made a neater job of it.

Finally, the C.I.D. had to admit themselves beaten, and I left the police station for the last time without a stain on my character. Huh! I lost my job, I lost my place of residence, I lost my friends. And, in addition to all this, no girl in that district would be seen dead with me. Though for weeks afterwards, had girls permitted me to escort them, they would have been the safest girls in the world. I never took a step without police protection, very, very unobtrusive. The smallest squeak would have brought the man on my tail to my side.

All the same, I wasn't moving from the neighborhood, not yet awhile. I found a fresh dwelling with a deaf mute for a landlady, a fresh job at half the pay, and there I stuck, waiting for time to pass which is reputedly a great healer.

But I was waiting with a purpose. When three months were up, I found myself alone again – without police protection, that is. Then I thought it was safe to get busy. They say a child's memory is short, and I didn't want to leave it too long. I started to hang about the Omega Road Girls' School, at four o'clock when the kids were coming out. I marked my prey; three months had made very little difference to her, and I herded her off from the rest of the flock. As a matter of fact, it was as easy as pie because she left the others at a road junction and trailed off on her own. I guess it was like that day at the pool; she was strictly an individualist. I had decided to use guile, and had been toting round with me for days a big bag of toffees.

'Hey, Ruby,' I said, catching up with her and offering the bag. 'Have a sweetie.'

She recognized me at once. She didn't look scared at all, but she shook her head and said, 'My mum says I'm never to take sweets from strangers.'

'I'm not a stranger. I'm the man you nearly put behind bars for life, don't you remember?'

'Serves yer right. You shouldn't have spoken nasty to me.'

Then she showed her teeth in the famous grin. You could see she didn't bear me an ounce of spite.

'Besides...' she said.

'Besides what?'

'I didn't want to get meself in trouble. I didn't want to draw attention to meself, see.'

My God, she'd got it all there in her little brain-pan at the age of eight or thereabouts. She didn't care a fig what became of me; it was her own skin she was intent on preserving.

She undoubtedly knew who had killed the girl...

I tried not to show any excitement, and I said as casually as I could, matching my step to hers: 'Then you saw the chap who did it. I thought it was one of your lies!'

'Don't be saucy. Of course I saw 'im. Leastways, I saw his back. He was bending over.'

'You mean you never saw his face at all. Well, that's no good, you couldn't pick him out.'

'I could and all, if I wanted to. Wears a blue suit.'

'So does my Uncle Bert. What the hell! Why every –'

'You shouldn't swear. My mum says it's not nice.'

'You and your mum! I'll tell you what your mum is, she's as big a liar as you are if she says you were at home minding the baby when you were busy snooping at people in the wood.'

'She can't keep her eye on the clock all the time, can she? Not with my young brother she can't. And I wasn't snooping, Mister Clever. I was playing 'ouses under the trees.'

'And you say you know this chap?'

I didden say I knew 'im. I said I could put my finger on 'im if I liked.'

'Then why don't you?'

'It's none of my business.' She brought it out with an air of secret triumph.

But it was my business all right, and my particular business to keep on baiting her until I got the response I wanted. I've often heard little girls doing it to each other, and nine times out of ten it works.

So I gathered my resources together and, packing all the scorn I could into my voice, said, 'Huh! Ruby Grant, you don't know a thing!'

'I do.'

'You're just making it up.'

'I'm not.'

'Yes, you are. You never saw the chap at all, or if you did, you wouldn't know him from Adam.'

'I told you 'e'd got blue clothes on.'

'Well, where does he live?'

'I dunno where 'e lives, but I know where 'e is this minnit.'

'You're a nasty story teller!'

'No, I'm not.'

'Yes, you are.'

I was thoroughly into the spirit of the thing, when she suddenly capitulated.,

'If I take you to where he is, then will you believe me?'

'Now you're talking,' I said. 'You take me to him and I'll believe you.'

She looked at me hard with that intent yet somehow vacant stare which was part of her make-up.

'If I do, will yer swear not to tell anyone?'

'Of course I will.'

'Then say it after me.';

'What is it? What have I got to say?'

She licked her grubby first finger and held it up in the air.

'See my finger's wet ... go on and say it.'

I licked my own finger and followed her instructions.

'See my finger's dry.'

'See my finger's dry.'

'Slit my throat if I tell a lie.' Here she drew her finger ominously across her scraggy little throat.

I repeated the childish oath. I hadn't the faintest intention of sticking to it. I'd have been an outright fool if I considered I owed any allegiance to that child.

But my having taken the oath seemed to satisfy her. She said, 'come on, then.'

She pranced off and I followed her as I'd done once before. The only difference was that now she wore a skimpy cloth coat and we were on the pavements and not in the path in the wood.

She led me from this by-road into another and yet another until at last we came out on the High Street. There were lots of people about shopping, but she didn't moderate her pace, but slipped between them like an eel, while I blundered after. I must have looked odd chasing after that scrap of a kid, as if life depended on it. But I wasn't conscious of making a fool of myself; my heart was thumping wildly, because I felt sure I was on to something important.

Finally, we came to the crossroads where the High Street joins the main arterial road coming from the city.

Ruby Grant came to a sudden standstill, which brought me right up on her heels.

She dropped back to my side, and looking up at me, gave the faintest flick to her thumb.

'There 'e is, then. What did I tell yer?'

There he was, with his back to us, blue suit, white gloves

and all, directing the home-going traffic, the young cop I'd given myself up to that day in the wood, by the paddling pool.

I stood gazing stupidly at him, my mind in a whirl, for perhaps ten seconds. Then I turned to Ruby. You know what? The little devil wasn't there. She'd played the same trick on me as before. She must have moved like greased lightning.

It was hopeless to look for her amongst the crowd. A child as small as that could take cover anywhere. She might have darted into the nearest chain store for temporary refuge, or be halfway home already.

So there I was, up a tree, I turned about and began to walk slowly back along the High Street, mechanically dodging the busy shoppers while I mulled what had happened over in my mind. Was Miss Ruby Gant stringing me along in her own inimitable fashion? And was this last audacity – pure invention on the spur of the moment – a final thumb at the nose at me, for venturing to criticize her past conduct?

Did her fiendish ingenuity prompt her to select a policeman as the supreme example of improbability? Was she even now giggling away at the idea of it?

Did she really know who had murdered the girl in the wood? Was the blue suit merely a product of her fertile fancy, or had it some basis in fact?

It was a matter beyond dispute that the cop had been right on the spot, or as near as makes no difference. It would have taken him less than no time to have slipped down the slope from the fatal tree into position as guardian of the pool. Just because no motive had come to light for the murder of the girl, it didn't follow that there was none.

When I was a boy I was never keen to tangle with the forces of law and order, and I could therefore imagine what effect the idea of mixing it with a policeman would have on one of Ruby's age and environment. You notice that I don't say tender age. Still, it was nice to think that there might be some reason for what that kid had done to me, besides the mere gratification of a childish spite.

Now that I harked back, I had a vivid mental picture of the blood draining out of the policeman's face when I first reported to him my discovery of the crime. Was every cop so squeamish, however inexperienced?

But even if Ruby had made me a present of the killer, what good was it likely to do me? I shouldn't like to see the expression on the sergeant's face if I'd be so foolish as to trot round to the police station with this new theory.

And suddenly I saw the whole thing from the point of view of the police, and knew myself that it was only a pack of lies, or rather, that mixture of truth and tarradiddle in which Ruby specialized.

Well, let bygones by bygones, I thought. Thanks to Ruby, I should always be a man with a past ... no need to allow her to complicate my future.

I felt that I needed a drink to strengthen my resolution, even if it was only a strong black coffee, and as this feeling happened to coincide with my passing one of the local milk bars, I pushed the door and went in.

It was one of those narrow affairs like a tramcar, with tables in front and the works at the end. I was nearly up to the counter when I saw something that pulled me up dead.

There, perched up on a stool, with her back three-quarters-wise to me, was that demon-child. She had her skinny elbows planted on the counter, and her monkey paws round a beakerful of something.

But she wasn't drinking. She seemed to be in a sort of ecstasy, gazing up with rapt adoration at the face of the Adonis presiding over the counter. The man was sleek and dark and as handsome as a rattlesnake. You know the type.

There was a loud sort of buzzing in my ears. I stood perfectly still, and deep down inside me I had that sudden hideous conviction of truth without proof such as a chap gets sometimes.

I added my stare to Ruby's.

The man must have just finished buttering some slices of cut bread ready for sandwiches, because he still held the knife loosely in his right hand, whilst with the index finger of the left he was absentmindedly testing the sharpness of the blade.

He was not interested in either of us.

All his attention was centered on the pair of young girls who sat at the table next to the counter, chattering away together in the animated way girls have if within ten yards of any personable male. His eyes, half-narrowed, feasted on them as on some delectable prospect.

Then, as if drawn by a magnet, he released the knife, and came forward, brushing past the entranced Ruby, to collect their empty cups.

As he bent over them in his regulation short white jacket, murmuring who knows what sweet inducements, he revealed to me the back view of a pair of pants of a peculiarly revolting shade. I decided not to stop for refreshment.

I did a rightabout turn, and was out of those surroundings in less time than it takes to say 'Blue Murder.'

Oh yes, I agree there are loose ends. There are several things I should like to know myself.

For instance, just when did Mistress Ruby catch up with him?

Did she track him down systematically by his choice in suiting? Had she known him before? Or was it one of those odd chances, beginner's luck, as you might say?

How long was he prepared to go on stuffing her up with free ice cream, hot chocolate and what have you, to keep her on his side?

And what was going to happen when he stopped?

Or when... well, never mind.

These questions, or any variants on same, are likely to go unanswered as far as I'm concerned.

When two tigers get together, that's no place for me.

Vacation

by Mike Brett

The motel was a luxurious U-shaped structure of redwood, aluminium and glass, two stories tall, the second floor having a continuous balcony that overlooked an enormous swimming pool. Charles and Lisa Hannaford arrived at one P.M. by taxi from the airport. In the warmth of the January sun the guests romped around the pool and relaxed on tubular beach chairs. They wore shorts and halters and swimsuits. Laughter and gay conversation drifted toward the Hannafords.

It was a Florida playground, and already Charles was beginning to feel some of his business tensions lift. The pool looked inviting. He wanted to change into his swimsuit, take a dip, then spend the rest of the day taking the sun.

They were going to stay a week. Perhaps tomorrow he would try his hand at a little golf, or perhaps Lisa would like to go out on a boat with him for some deep-sea fishing.

Lisa caught his arm. 'It's beautiful, Charles, isn't it?' she said, smiling.

'Yes, it's lovely.' He never ceased to be amazed at her beauty. She was thirty-two now, and they had been married eight years. It was ten years since his first wife had died, and he had raised his two sons by himself until he had married Lisa. Twenty years older than Lisa, he was aware of her freshness and her enthusiasm, and the never-ending delight of looking at her.

In their room, they changed to swim suits, and he kissed her. 'You're right again,' he said. 'I'm glad we came down here.'

Taking the vacation had been her idea. He owned a real estate firm. A big one, and he worked hard. But lately the big deals had fallen through, and some of the smaller ones, too, had gone sour. He'd come home tired and irritable. Competition had sprung up all round him over the years, and every day had been a battle.

It hadn't affected his love for Lisa, however. The wonder and the magic were still there for him. At night, alone in their bedroom, he had watched her brushing her long, black hair, and he knew she was the richness of his life.

But the strain of business had begun to take its toll from him. There were too many nights when he hadn't left the office until midnight. He smoked too much, he drank too many martinis, and he had put on too much weight.

The odds had been stacked heavily against their marriage from the beginning. Some of his best friends had warned him against marrying her. Of course, they had all been tactful. 'You don't marry a girl with her background, Charlie,' they had said. None of them had actually come right out and labeled her.

While driving over a bridge on his way home one rainy evening, he had seen her climb to the rail, poised to leap into the dark waters. She was twenty-four years old then, already so filled with her own feeling of futility that she no longer wanted to live.

But Charles Hannaford had seen something in the girl, had painstakingly gone about the business of convincing her she was a valuable human being, and had asked her to marry him. After much persuasion, he had convinced her that he was a very lonely man, and that she would indeed brighten his home.

A nice home, small circle of friends (some hadn't accepted her) and the warm security of being truly loved by Charles Hannaford had made her a functioning human being. They'd had eight good years, and he thought she was lovelier than when he had married her.

Lisa had seen the pressure on him these last few months, and had insisted upon the vacation. The strain was there with good cause. He was fifty-two years old. The ugly specter of failure loomed before him. It didn't make sense to leave a business that was going bad, for pleasure. But now he was happy they had taken the vacation. Somehow, Lisa's optimism was contagious.

The trouble really started when they left their room for the pool. From the narrow balcony skirting the second floor of the motel, a blond giant of heroic dimensions called, 'Lisa, honey!' then dove toward the pool. In those few seconds, Charles had seen a look of fear come over Lisa's face.

'Is there anything wrong?' he asked. 'You're as white as a sheet.'

'No. I'm all right. I knew him, Charles. I spent some time in Florida, ten years ago. We can leave if you like,' she added meaningfully. 'I think it would be better if we did.'

'No. We're staying. We don't run from anything, Lisa,' he said gently.

The man in the pool climbed out, dripping water. He was tall and his muscles bulged, a weight lifter, a physical fitness man. With his long blond hair and his deeply tanned body, he might have been a Viking god.

He stepped up to Lisa as though he had seen her only yesterday, and placed his hand on her arm. 'Lisa, honey! Where you been? I recognized you the minute I set eyes on you.' He spoke to her, but his eyes measured Hannaford speculatively.

'This is my husband,' she said quickly, and Charles detected the nervousness. 'My husband, Charles Hannaford,' emphasizing it. 'I don't seem to remember your name,' she said weakly.

Charles felt an emphatic reaction. He felt his wife's discomfort. This was the first time anything like this had occured since they were married. Her past had come up out of nowhere. There was no running away now. The blond giant, standing before her, blocked the sunlight from her. His shadow covered her like an evil embrace.

The light-haired man stood with his feet spread apart and his hands on his hips, confidently. 'It's natural, your forgetting my name, Lisa,' he said and smiled. 'I'm Bill Rennie. It's been a long time, and you knew a lot of people when you were down here. Got a cigarette?' he said casually.

Charles handed one to him and lit it for him.

Rennie stared at Lisa boldly. Then the thin lips smiled knowingly. 'It's been a long time, but it sure is nice seeing you again. You look terrific, just terrific.' His eyes swept over her body. He chuckled. 'Put on a couple of pounds since I saw you last. I remember you as a real thin kid.' He extended his hand to Charles. 'You're a lucky man,' he said. 'Real lucky.'

Charles could sense the mockery in his tone. 'Thank you, I feel that way too.'

Bill turned to Lisa. 'Guess you were kind of surprised to see me flying through the air like that. I get all the guests shook up every time they see it. They don't expect to see anybody flying down from up there.' He winked at her. 'Remember me, baby? I was always the high flier in the crowd.'

'Yes,' she said. 'I remember you.'

He pounded a large hand against his stomach. 'Still in great shape.' He pointed up to the balcony. 'I got it made. I live up there, in room fifteen. I get up in the morning and take off like a bird. Never have used the stairs to get down to the pool. That's strictly for tourists. We natives know better. How long you folks going to stick around?'

'A week,' Charles said.

Lisa said quickly, 'Perhaps a day.'

'No,' Bill said. 'You'll stay longer than that. This is a terrific place. It'll take a week just to get comfortable.' He glanced at Lisa again and said, 'Mr. Hannaford, you sure picked yourself a winner.'

'Yes, I think so,' Charles said amiably.

Bill flicked the ash off the end of his cigarette. 'Why don't you folks drop up to my place tonight? I'm having a party. Some of the locals and some of the tourists. We have a ball. You can come anyway you like. Shorts, bathings suits, or evening dress – anything you like, as long as you're comfortable. Me, I wear swim trunks.'

'I don't know,' she said lamely. 'I don't think we'll be able to make it. We've just come down and the long trip –'

'Oh, come on,' Bill said cheerfully. 'It'll be like old times, Lisa. We've got plenty to talk over, and you'll have a good time too, sir,' he said to Charles.

'I'm sure I will,' Hannaford replied. 'We'll be there. Thank you, we'd like to come.' Rennie's *sir* had made him feel older.

'Swell,' said Bill. 'We start around twelve o'clock. Don't do much sleeping around here, you know.'

Charles watched Rennie's shoulders as he walked away, the deeply tanned body, the long blond hair, and the swaggering walk.

'I don't want to go,' Lisa said very softly.

'We don't have to,' he replied gently. 'But I think we should.'

Her face was flushed. 'You saw him, you saw the way he looked at me.'

He nodded his head slowly. 'He's wrong. He's looking at something in the past.'

'That's the way he remembers it.' She touched his elbow. 'We don't have to stay here, Charles. There are so many places where we can stay, with more privacy.'

'One place isn't any different than the rest. The only important thing is you.'

'Then let's get out of here, Charles. Honestly, I want to leave. Staying here is unfair to you.' She turned her head away and her voice was very quiet. 'I was dirt when I knew him. You heard him, and you saw the way he looked at me. He makes me feel dirty.'

He shook his head. 'We're staying.' The knowing innuendoes in the man's tone still rankled.

'What are you trying to prove?' she asked angrily.

'Nothing, nothing at all. That's just the point. We don't have to prove anything.'

'Thank you,' she said, and he felt a pang of sympathy as she forced a smile. 'He won't let up, Charles.'

He shook his head soberly, a stocky, solid man. 'He doesn't know with whom he's dealing. I do.'

'I love you, Charles,' she said simply. Then she ran from him, and he saw her body knife the air as she dove into the pool. She was an excellent swimmer. He barely managed to stay afloat.

He went in after a while, for a few minutes, then came out and dried in the sun. He listened to the roar of conversation and laughter around the pool, the squealing horseplay of children, the exclamations of card players.

He stretched out on a beach chair and shut his eyes against the strong rays of the sun. A running child, dripping pool water, made him sit up. On the other side of the pool, he could see Lisa and Bill Rennie, side by side, dangling their legs in the water. The man was laughing, and even from this distance, across the pool, Charles could see a pained expression on Lisa's face.

Real brave man, Charles told himself, a hero. You're fifty-two years old, and you throw her right into the path of a guy who can put pressure on her.

He watched Lisa smile at Bill.

How smart are you, Hannaford? he asked himself. You've married her and you've already beaten the odds. What more do you want? But to turn and run now would be an admission of his lack of faith in her. It would destroy what they had built up between them.

Later, they dined at the motel's restaurant, overlooking the pool, and she was quiet and thoughtful. The pool had been emptied of guests and a handyman was cleaning an oily film from the side of the pool with a big brush.

They strolled for a while after dinner, then went back to their room. They were both very tired, and she suggested they take a nap. He went to bed. He heard her moving about in the room, then he heard the soft murmuring of the shower. A little while later, he heard her come out of the shower, and she sat down and brushed her hair.

Charles fell asleep. He awakened to darkness and the steady hum of the air conditioner. He was alone. Lisa was gone. He could feel the acceleration of his heartbeat. He lay there in an agony of torment.

Then he heard the key in the lock. Without knowing why, he shut his eyes and pretended he was asleep. She came into the room stealthily, taking one slow step after another. He felt the bed give as she lay down beside him, and then he heard her quick breathing. In the darkness of the room, he felt sick.

After a while she got up and dressed. He must have dozed off again, he realized, when she shook him and awakened him. It was a quarter to twelve.

She was wearing a shimmering white evening dress. Her hair was beautifully combed. Her neck was white and strong, and her lips were full and red.

'Come on,' she said and smiled. 'We're going to a party. You'll probably want to put on a sport jacket.'

The party was already in full swing when they arrived.

Hollywood's version of the lover, Bill Rennie, greeted them. Charles could see the quick glint of amusement in Rennie's eyes. The guests had come as he had said. There were perhaps fifteen people in the room, and their dress ranged from cocktail dresses to slacks and swimsuits. There were lovely women here, Charles saw. But none lovelier than his wife. He felt an inexplicable sense of sadness.

The guests danced to the music of an ancient record player, set off in a corner. Bill danced with an assortment of happy, smiling women. And then he was dancing with Lisa, holding her tight. He kept whispering into her ear.

By three A.M., a good percentage of the guests were drunk. One intense, dark-haired girl had a crying jag. She loved her boss; alas, he loved his wife.

Charles watched his wife dancing with Rennie. He saw her nod to something Rennie had said. She left Rennie quickly and walked over to him. Her blue eyes were enormous in her curiously pale face.

'I'm going back to our room for a while,' she said softly. 'I have to get something, and I want to put on fresh lipstick.'

'Sure,' he said. 'Sure.'

He made himself another drink, but he knew that all the whiskey here wasn't going to rid him of the bitter taste in his mouth.

Out in the center of the room, Bill Rennie suddenly pretended to be very drunk. He had been cold sober up to this point. He staggered a bit and made a drunken announcement. 'Good-bye, cruel world,' he said, then climbed up on the open window and stood poised, ready to dive.

Cries of panic burst from those who had never seen him jump into the pool from his room, and wild laughter from those who had.

Charles caught a glimpse of Bill's face, saw the mockery in it. It was all there before him now. Lisa was already gone; now Bill Rennie was going to join her. He was going to jump into the pool, and guests were going to scream and expect to see his crushed body down below.

Bill Rennie was going to meet his wife somewhere. Charles had gambled and he had lost. Never had he felt so old, tired.

Bill Rennie dove out over the balcony toward the pool, his

grandstand trick. Some of the guests scrambled to the window. A woman screamed, but it was mock screaming. There were too many guests around her who were calm. It was a gag of some kind.

Suddenly, from below, near the pool, another woman began to scream. It split the night, and lights began to go on all over the place.

Men began to run from all directions. They pulled Bill Rennie out of the pool and stretched him out while they waited for an ambulance to arrive.

He was alive. Both arms were broken, and there was a severe cut over his head. His face would never be the same.

One of the men who had pulled him out of the pool said, 'He's lucky. There's still about three feet of water in the deep part of the pool. That's all that saved his life.'

The police arrived with sirens blasting the night. They investigated and found that some joker had opened both drain cocks and had almost emptied the pool.

'It must have happened early in the evening,' the hotel manager volunteered. 'It would take several hours for the level to drop this much.'

Charles Hannaford walked slowly back to his hotel room. Several hours for the pool's level to drop; that was about the time he had fallen asleep that night, right after dinner.

Charles entered his room very quietly. A small lamp was lit, and he could see his lovely wife, sleeping. Did he imagine it, or was there a tiny smile around her mouth?

Charles bent over her and kissed her, and felt a heady sense of triumph. You have to fight to keep what you have.

A Flower for Her Grave

by Hilda Cushing

It was just nine when Matt Lucas turned off the station lights and snapped the lock on the office door. He went to the small room in the rear where he used to keep supplies, but where he now lived, sleeping on the cot in the corner and cooking his meals on the two-burner hot plate. He changed from his coveralls into fresh chinos, plaid shirt and a windbreaker, and taking the flowers he had picked earlier in the evening, he let himself out the back door.

His car stood in the garage near the grease pit. Although it had been secondhand when he bought it in July, it was in excellent condition. The few nicks in the grillwork were not too obvious and it had been simple enough for him to pound out the dents in the fenders. After he had overhauled the motor, it purred as though it were fresh from the factory.

He had owned the station for a little over a year. After his retirement from the Stevenwell factory, compulsory at sixty-five, it had seemed a natural transition to own a service station which was complete with a garage for minor repairs and small parts. Both he and his wife were healthy and energetic, and had felt it was something they could handle together without hiring outside help. Although the hours were long and seven days a week, the road was only moderately traveled.

There had been plenty of time for Alethea to cultivate the garden in front of the station, to keep the little house next door, to cook appetizing meals, and to spell Matt at the gas pumps whenever he wanted a break. Coupled with the pension from the plant, it was a satisfactory living.

Alethea had been dead three months. So Matt had sold the little house and moved into the rear room of the station. It was lonely with his wife gone but it seemed less so away from the house that cried out her absence.

He was careful with the flowers as he laid them on the seat beside him. They were fall mums that his wife had planted in the spring, gay and perky like herself.

There were no green thumbs on Matt but he kept the garden watered and free from weeds, and every Saturday he picked the prettiest of whatever was in blossom. The cemetery was fifteen miles away, in Mason City, but because he opened later on Sundays than on other days, he could still get in the full night's sleep he needed.

Fortunately, the station was in Stevenwell where he had lived most of his life. His old friends went out of their way to get their gas from him, and his new neighbors were kind. The men stopped often to chat with him and the women brought him treats for his meals.

Lately, Sergeant Paul Graham of the state police was in the habit of dropping by. Riding around most of the time, he used a lot of gas. Sometimes the cruiser needed emergency repairs. Sometimes he stopped just to talk. His frequent visits helped the time pass until it was Saturday night again.

As always, after dark, the entrance to the cemetery was chained so Matt parked his car by the side of the road and walked the hundred yards or so to Alethea's grave. Because of the thin clouds across the moon, its light shone soft and mellow on the small gray stone.

Matt threw the remains of last week's flowers in the trash bin nearby. There was no perpetual care here, and now, the middle of October, the water had been turned off until spring.

Along with the flowers and the water Matt had brought a cushion. The night air made the ground damp and lately he had noticed a stiffness whenever he bent his knees. He sat for a few moments looking around the cemetery. It seemed nicer tonight. The clouds blurred the neglected and unkempt plots. Some of the stones were large but many, like Alethea's, were of modest size. Most had dates of birth and death, while several of the larger ones had a phrase or a verse chipped into them.

His wife's stone had only 'Alethea' on it. It was a pretty name, an endearment in itself, and he loved to say it. The last name was unimportant. There was only Matt. There were no children, and all their close relatives were gone. It would never matter to anyone but himself where her grave was.

After the few moments of orientation. Matt began to talk. He was a simple, unimaginative man. He didn't believe in ghosts or spirits, or that the soul stayed with the body after death; but he was lonely and because her body was in the grave at his feet and because of the name on the stone, he felt near to her here.

During their thirty-eight years of marriage, they had never been separated except for that one time – the two weeks just before her death – the two weeks she had spent in her old home town of Wortham, seventy-six miles upstate, attending to the last days and burial of her only remaining relative, her sister, Miriam. Always before, Matt had accompanied her on her visits to Wortham; the station had made that impossible this last time.

Matt sat on his pillow, his short legs stretched out from his chunky body, his head bent a little, and, like every other Saturday night, he talked to his dead wife who had been short, too, and plump, and whose plain face had always appeared happy and loving.

'Sergeant Graham, the state trooper I told you about, stopped by again this morning, Alethea. Nothing new. He's on the late shift this month. Mavis – that's his wife – is going to have another baby. He says that makes three. In December sometime, they expect it.'

He paused between thoughts.

'Mrs. Cunningham brought over some stew for supper. It was pretty spicy and I couldn't eat much of it, but she meant well so I threw away what was left before she sent one of her children over for the dish.'

He shifted his legs a little.

'Got a letter from that lawyer who's handling Miriam's estate. The house brought a few thousand. She left everything to you – so now it comes to me. It will help. Won't have to paint the place myself. Need a few tools. Perhaps I'll get someone in to help over the weekends. Perhaps some boy from the high school.'

That would please her. Alethea liked young people. This swing, mod, hip or whatever they called it generation never irritated her the way it did Matt. She used to say they only took a 'little understanding', but Matt had no tolerance for the restless, brash types who roared up to the pumps in their souped-up heaps.

Somewhere in Stevenwell there must be some well brought up, ambitious boy who would like to make a little money in a part-time job; someone like the son they had wanted and never had. Perhaps he ought to talk it over with the sergeant before he contacted the high school, he told Alethea. Graham had lived in Stevenwell all his life. He should know who was headed for trouble and who wasn't. The town was small enough for that.

'Mrs. Hooper,' he continued, 'you must remember her, the big wheel in the garden club with the Pontiac I got the dent out of when she hit the hydrant in front of Penney's? Remember, she told you her husband never found out! Well, she says I should cover the garden after the first hard frost. Showed me which ones come up every year and promised to bring some annuals in the spring.'

His pause here was long and ended in an explosive, 'It's not easy, Alethea – not easy at all – this living alone! I miss you so much!'

He swallowed hard. Only three months, and he was breaking his basic rule: to remain calm and cheerful during these visits.

'But I'm all right!' he promised hastily. 'Don't you worry one bit! Keeping busy does the trick and I haven't grown sloppy either. I keep the sheets changed and the wash done. Still go every week to the all-night laundromat.' He rubbed his forehead as though it ached but it was just a mannerisim he had acquired lately. 'Think I'll add on space for a shower stall before I get the station painted.'

He could see Alethea smiling at this. Just last week he had regaled her with the unpredictability of the garden hose when it was attached to the faucet in the lavatory for his early morning shower.

He sat awhile without saying anything. There was a chill in the air. He'd better wear a pair of woolen pants next week instead of chinos.

'Oh, yes,' he roused himself. 'Don't think I'll close up all day this Thanksgiving, the way we did last year when Miriam came down. A few hours, perhaps. Mrs. Cunningham has invited me to dinner. A whole month away and she invited me already!' he chuckled. 'She sure is nice but she's a terrible cook! Guess she can't do much harm to a turkey though.' Then he added, 'Want to bet?'

The chuckle threatened to turn into a sob. He choked it back. He sat there for a while longer, then leaned forward to loosen the stems of the flowers in the container. Alethea liked them floppy. She said they were more natural that way.

'Well, Alethea,' he said, heaving himself to his feet, 'guess that's about all the news I got this time.'

He looked around slowly and wondered what it was going to be like in the winter. Would he be able to get through the snow after a big storm? He shook his head as though to clear it. He wasn't one to worry ahead of time. He would take each Saturday night as it came.

The car started easily, as usual. There was very little traffic along the road at this time of night. Sometimes he met or was passed by a car or two just over the Stevenwell line where the shortcut to the turnpike from Route 113 joined it. Now and then there would be a hitchhiker on his way to the entrance of the toll road interchange where it was fairly simple to pick up a ride.

Matt rounded the last sharp corner and was within two miles of the station when he saw him. Matt's car lights swinging around the curve had alerted him and in two quick strides he had swung himself to the center of the road, with right arm and thumb extended, and with that cocksure, confident grin they all seemed to have. He was probably around twenty, skinny, and with hair that fell like a mop over his forehead.

He was only a short distance from the turn and he held his ground until the car was almost upon him. Then just as he was about to step back and just as the grin began to fade, Matt gunned the motor and caught the thumber with such force that he was tossed into the air before he hit the macadam.

Matt backed up a few feet before he got out of his car. The

boy was dead, probably from a broken neck. Matt dragged the body to the grass at the side of the road where the overhanging branches from the bushes would hide it, at least until daylight.

There was damage to the front of the car but not so much as last time. The grillwork, alone, had caught the impact, and the fresh dent from the slight weight of the boy was camouflaged by the many already there. The headlight was intact. He wouldn't have to take time to pick up each piece of glass, which was always hazardous. Another car might come along.

Something had flown out from under the boy's left arm as he was hit. Matt crossed the road to find it. It was a large thick book, shabby from use and scored by gravel; obviously a college textbook, something about electronics on the cover. He tossed it over the stone wall that edged that side of the road and stood a few moments biting his lip.

When he started back to the car, he was still somewhat bemused and the lights and the auto were around the bend and upon him before he could reach safety.

The driver stopped. Matt could just barely hear voices. The masculine one: 'He may still be alive. Get back in the car and get help – get the police. I'll wait here!'

A woman's voice, frantic: 'Don't you realize what that will mean? My husband will find out! We've got to get away from here! Right away! Hurry!'

There was a moment of silence, the sound of doors slamming, gears shifting, and the revving of the motor as the car skirted his body and the driver and his companion raced away. They hadn't been as lucky as Matt. Pieces of their broken headlight lay on the road, sparkling in the moonlight.

Sergeant Graham tiptoed up the stairs and into the bedroom. Mavis, his wife, in her seventh month, needed her sleep.

It was no good. She awoke as she always did. The light flashed on before he could close the door behind him. She pushed her pillow up against the headboard, her face flushed like a child's, her hair tousled.

'You're late, Paul,' she said, not accusingly but with a hint of resignation.

'Another hit and run,' he answered laconically as he got out of his uniform. 'DOA.'

'Another!' She was wide awake now. 'And on a Saturday again. How many does that make?'

'Six since the middle of July and all on the same stretch of road between Mason City and Stevenwell.'

From habit he undressed swiftly. He was in his pajamas now.

'Anyone from around here?' She was surprised when he nodded. The others had all been from distant places.

'Old Matt Lucas – owns the gas station over on Center Street.'

'For heaven's sake!' She sat up straight. Her eyes were filled with concern. 'The poor man! What was he doing walking along that road at night?'

'We haven't figured it out. We got this anonymous call from a pay phone around eleven. When we got there, his car was at the side of the road and he was near the middle. Must have been on his way home from the cemetery in Mason city. He was in the habit of going there Saturday nights.' He hung his uniform carefully in the closet. His voice was somewhat muffled but Mavis could still hear him. 'There was broken glass nearby – has to be a headlight. Maybe this time we'll be able to trace it. About time for a break.'

'That poor man,' said Mavis again. 'Didn't he lose his wife a while ago?' She thought for a moment. 'Wasn't she murdered?'

Paul slipped into bed beside her. 'On the way home from burying her sister in Wortham, three months back.'

'I remember!' Mavis turned out the light and wriggled her bulky body down beside her husband. 'You found her and the car three days later in the Lakeville woods near the reservoir – strangled and her purse missing!'

'Right.' The sergeant was tired but he knew his wife. She had to have it straighted out in her mind or she'd never get to sleep or let him.

'But you never found who did it!'

'No, not yet anyway.' It had been a long night but his voice was patient. 'We're still working on it but we've never had any but the one clue. Someone who knew her saw her stop her car just outside of Wortham to pick up a hitchhiker.'

Another Beautiful Day

by Harold Dutch

If I'd driven into town at midnight in the midst of a thunderstorm, with flashes of lightning and claps of thunder, it would be easier for me to believe what happened. If I'd driven in on a bleak October day, with the cold wind from the sea blowing dead leaves along deserted streets, I might have sensed what was to come. As it was, I drove into Bellport on a bright, hot summer afternoon, the harbor waters sparkling with sunshine and covered with pleasure craft, the homes – both year-round and summer – attractive and inviting, and the streets busy with happy, friendly-looking people.

It had been almost seven years since I'd driven up the Maine coast to Bellport. The trip was pleasant, and I took longer than I should have, for I was not exactly looking forward to visiting with Aunt Sarah. Since the tragedy that so affected all of us, her mind tends to wander and dwell on unpleasant things. This is what I was told by the woman I'd hired to care for her, for I hadn't seen Aunt Sarah since that night. Mrs. Record, the companion and housekeeper, wrote to me perhaps twice a month, a page at the most, but enough to keep me informed about my only living relative.

For years the trip to Bellport to visit Aunt Sarah and Uncle Hiram had been such a joy, at least for my brother and me, then to wander through the large house, up and down the stairways, hide in the huge closets, play in the great barn and its loft, pore over what seemed hundreds of old picture albums and the treasures that Uncle Hiram had brought back from all over the world.

Uncle Hiram was the object of our greatest affection. He seemed like a giant of a man to us in those days, tall, rugged, with a mass of untamed hair over a ruddy and creased face that featured a beak of a nose, redder than the rest of his face, and dancing blue eyes. Uncle Hiram was always ready to play with us, always had some new, gory adventure tale that supposedly happened to him in some far-away place or on one of the many vessels he sailed. It wasn't until we were in high school that my brother and I realized what a low opinion our parents had of Uncle Hiram.

Aunt Sarah was mother's sister; Bellport was their hometown; and the house had been their father's, a well-known sea captain. Mother married an insurance man from Rhode Island. Aunt Sarah, late in life, married the gay seadog – a union, I found out later, that was frowned on by her family and most people in town. The opinion was that Uncle Hiram married Aunt Sarah for her money. She was locally prominent, quite well off, and had a fine home. He had spent his life roaming the world on all types of ships, had never been more than an able-bodied seaman with none too solid a reputation, but he had a charm and a personality few could resist. He gave up the sea when he married Aunt Sarah and settled down to look after his business interests, although few knew exactly what those interests were.

For as long as I can remember, each summer, during Dad's vacation, we came up – or 'down' as Mother and Aunt Sarah used to say – for our yearly visit. My brother and I were identical twins: Donald and Ronald.

We drove through town, took the road that circled the bay, and soon could see the house on Height Of Land, looking down on the jagged rocks, the calm waters, and across to Bellport. The house, like so many in these Maine coastal towns, was white with green jalousie shutters, with a widow's walk perched atop the main part of the three-story house. It faced the bay and stood perhaps five hundred feet from the cliff. The drop was about thirty feet. At high tide, the water came to the base of the rock; at low tide, a rocky bottom was exposed, and here we often dug for clams. Steep and rickety wooden steps led down to the water level and a float, where Uncle Hiram kept a dinghy. There was a small lawn in front of the house, the rest being hay field, except for a small grove of pines clinging to the high point of the cliff. The road ran back of the house and its long, two-story ell. The big barn, painted red, stood on the right of the house and close to the road. A two-car garage, which Uncle Hiram had added in later years, was on the left of the house and connected to the 'back room,' as we called it – the end room in the ell.

Now I pulled into the driveway, and before I got out of the car Aunt Sarah was standing in the doorway. She must have been watching for me. She held out her arms, and I could see the tears running down her cheeks. She held me tightly for some time, her head on my shoulder. Aunt Sarah was short and heavy, with a round face that had lost none of its fullness and was still free from wrinkles. She must have been seventy-three, at least. As I remembered, she was ten years older than Mother. Her short white hair, a little too blue in shade, was in frizzy curls. She had probably had someone come in to 'do' it in anticipation of my visit.

Aunt Sarah finally looked up into my face, then kissed me on the cheek. 'Thank you for coming, Ronald,' she said. 'It's been so long.'

I patted her on the shoulder. 'And it's nice to see you, Aunt Sarah. But I'm Donald.'

A wild, mad look came into her eyes. It frightened me, and I tried to pull away, but she held me tight, staring wide-eyed at me. Then suddenly, the eyes became blank, and she released me.

'Yes. Yes, of course,' she said. 'Come in and meet Mrs. Record.'

She took my hand and led me through the back room, with its laundry equipment, stacks of flowerpots, old sweaters and aprons hung on wall hooks, with rubbers and overshoes beneath, assorted hand tools scattered over an old scarred chest of drawers, and numerous other items filling every corner. The room hadn't changed for as long as I could remember, except for the modern laundry equipment. We went through the pantry, its shelves well stocked, and through the large kitchen with its table in the center of the room, through the dining room with its large and ornate furniture, including sideboard and china closet, and into the parlor at the front of the house.

Aunt Sarah led me to Mrs. Record who was seated in a chair by the window, knitting. 'Alma, this is my nephew, Donald. My sister's boy. Donald, this is Mrs. Record, who was nice enough to come in and stay with me.'

We said hello and Mrs. Record sadly shook her head.

'I know Mrs. Record,' I said to Aunt Sarah. 'I got her to come stay here with you, remember?'

She just patted my hand and said, 'Come and sit on the couch with me and tell me all about yourself. What have you been doing?'

This room, too, looked the same as it always had – crowded. Although a large, high-posted room, it pressed in on you with the hundreds of items it contained: chairs, tables, nicknack shelves, pictures, the heavy upholstered furniture with its crocheted antimacassars, the big fireplace, the great windows surrounded with heavy draperies. Every bit of floor and wall space seemed occupied, and the tables, the shelves, and the fireplace mantel were covered with framed snapshots, figurines, plates.

'I'm still with the bank,' I said. 'You know that. I write, you, but I never hear from you.'

She sighed. 'Oh, it's so hard for me to settle down and write. I've asked Alma to write you. Doesn't she?'

Mrs. Record said, 'Now, Mrs. Spinney, I read you every letter I write to him. And I always ask you if there is anything special you want me to say, don't I?'

I changed the subject. 'You're looking very well, Aunt Sarah. Do you get out much?'

'I get out and tend my flowers when the weather's warm. We go over town shopping most every week. But I haven't been out the past few days. Those men have been around here, and I . . .' Her voice faded.

I looked at Mrs. Record. 'FBI,' she said. 'They're still looking for it.'

'You never mentioned it in your letters.'

'They just showed up a few days ago. They want to find it before the seven years are up, don't they?'

Aunt Sarah patted my hand again and smiled at me as if she hadn't heard us. 'You look about the same, Ron –

Donald. Why didn't Nellie and Philip come with you?'

Mrs. Record and I exchanged glances again. 'Mother and Dad died, remember?'

She looked at me a moment with that blank stare, then sighed. 'Oh, yes. Yes, the same time Hiram went. I saw him the other night.'

Mrs. Record dropped her knitting in her lap. 'Now, Mrs. Spinney, you know you didn't see anyone!'

'But I did, dear. As plain as I see you.'

Mrs. Record said to me, 'She thought she heard something night before last and went wandering out in the hall. I heard her calling and got her back in bed. There was no one around, and I didn't hear a thing except her.'

'I know I saw Hiram. He was going up the stairs to the third floor. That's why I called to him, but he just disappeared.'

'Aunt Sarah,' I said. I felt she must face the truth. 'Aunt Sarah, listen to me carefully. Uncle Hiram, my father, and Ronald were all killed, all the same night, almost seven years ago now. And the shock killed Mother the next day – her heart. You, too, were in the hospital – for a month or so. You remember that, don't you?'

She was looking out of the window, down toward the bay. 'I don't see the men today. Yesterday, they were searching all over the field and cliff.'

Mrs. Record rolled her eyes and got up from the chair. 'Well, I'll get supper. We eat around here at five o'clock,' she said to me, 'if you don't mind. Supper at five, bed at nine.'

'I don't mind a bit. I didn't have much lunch, so I'm hungry.'

'Good. We're having lobster salad. Your Aunt Sarah remembered you liked that.'

'Wonderful!' I turned to Aunt Sarah. 'Thank you very much.'

Aunt Sarah was staring into space, smiling to herself. She murmured something.

The supper was truly delicious, the lobster fresh from the sea water at the lobster pound down the road, and Mrs. Record's sourmilk biscuits, the flakiest and lightest I'd ever eaten, so hot from the oven the butter immediately became rivulets. Aunt Sarah had wanted to eat in the dining room, in my honor, but I insisted we sit at the kitchen table. This is where we'd always eaten, except when special guests came. It was a bright, cheerful room, and I thoroughly enjoyed the meal.

We chatted pleasantly on a number of things unrelated to the family, and Aunt Sarah was rational throughout the meal; in fact, through the evening. She took me outside and showed me her flower beds, told me all her troubles with weeds and the bugs, what insecticides she used, how often she watered, and just what fertilizer was best. It was warm, so we sat outside until dark. The harbor was a busy place on a summer evening, with many pleasure craft plying the waters and a number out fishing. There were rowboats, outboards of all sizes, lobster boats, sailboats, and cabin cruisers. I felt very relaxed, and the fear of my visit disappeared.

Shortly after we came inside, Aunt Sarah and Mrs. Record went to bed. I sat up for a while looking over the old picture albums, the ones that covered the years of our visits. Here were Aunt Sarah and Uncle Hiram holding us as babies; Aunt Sarah holding both of us; Uncle Hiram holding both. Here we were on top of a hay wagon, with Dad and Uncle Hiram standing beside the horse. There was a snap of us sitting on the hood of the new Essex Dad had bought just before vacation. Two out-of-focus shots were labeled: 'Donald taken by Ronald' and 'Ronald taken by Donald.' Here we were at a clambake. Written on it was: 'Ronald with the Lobster. Donald with the Hamburger.' There was one of me standing on the stairway platform at the top of the cliff, taken by my brother. This picture had been a great joke with us, because there I was standing on our secret hiding place, and no one could see it. We had dug up a large sod by the side of the platform and, over a period of days, handful by handful, scooped out the earth beneath the planks and scattered it over the cliff. With the sod of tall grass in place, no one could tell there was an empty space under the platform. We had dug a large hole, and here we hid many of our treasures, and never told anyone. I remembered how many times we showed that picture, giggling the while because no one suspected our secret.

I flipped the pages of the album, and the years passed. On

each few pages we grew a little older. Here we were with two girls, standing at the front of the house. It was the summer after our first year at college. They were Bellport girls we'd invited to a dance, daughters of some friends of Aunt Sarah's. She wanted a picture of us 'all dressed up,' so we brought the girls to the house and posed self-consciously on the granite steps. The girls were wearing white dresses with flared skirts. The length looked ridiculous now. And we were in white jackets, with gray flannels. I smiled. We looked so young, so innocent, but that night our education was to begin.

We went to a dance pavilion at a lake. It had a wide veranda all around, with the sides of the building open to the night. A huge lighted globe of multi-colored glass, hung from the center of the ceiling, went 'round and 'round, splattering the floor with dots of red, blue, green, yellow. We danced until one o'clock to 'Route 66,' 'Ole Buttermilk Sky,' 'Civilization (Bongo, Bongo, Bongo),' 'Five Minutes More,' and other late hits I can't remember.

We got back to the house, after taking the girls home, about two A.M. We walked around the house to go in the front door, as it was closer to our bedroom, when we saw the figure down by the cliff. It was a dark night, under a pale, new moon, but at regular intervals a shadow at the top of the stairs was outlined against the bay, then it would disappear down the steps or into the blackness of the field. We watched for a while, saying nothing. A man seemed to be carrying something heavy up the steps and going back empty-handed.

I felt a nudge in my ribs. I nodded and slowly we started down through the fields. It was early July, and the hay had not been cut. The rustle of the grass seemed thunder to our ears, and we stopped every few steps to make sure we were not heard. It seemed to take us forever, and I wished I hadn't come. Across the bay an occasional light twinkled, but almost everyone in Bellport was in bed. Once, a moving glare indicated a car on the road. We could hear its engine as it started up the hill toward the house. The figure, at that moment at the cliff's edge, stopped and turned. We ducked down in the grass. The sound of the car grew louder, the lights brighter, then they passed the house and faded in the distance. We both sighed ad cautiously stood up. The figure was gone, and we picked our way on down. We could now hear the lapping of the water on the rocks. It would be almost high tide. We ducked again as the shadow came up to the top, carrying a box or a chest. I had visions of pirate's treasure and hidden gold. A few feet from the platform, he put the box down. There were a number of them lined up. We moved to the left to get into the pine grove, then on the soft pine needles ran to the edge and looked down. A lobster boat was tied up to the float. I was wondering where the man was when I felt the big hand on my shoulder. I jumped, and must confess I yelled. The hand slapped over my mouth, and a deep voice said, 'Be quiet, laddie. You want to wake the dead?'

It was Uncle Hiram!

He took his hand off my mouth. 'If you laddies want to go sneaking about in the dark of night, take off your fancy white jackets. You stand out like a sore thumb. Now, how about bed? I'll walk halfway up with you.' He took each of us by the arm in a strong grip and led us through the grove, carefully avoiding, I noticed, getting too close to those boxes, or whatever they were.

Trying to be nonchalant, I asked him. 'What are you doing out so late, Uncle Hiram?'

'Tending to a little business. You boys didn't know, but I do a little importing on the side. The shipment happened to come in a little late.'

Ronald suddenly broke from Uncle Hiram's grasp, then calmly walked over to the mysterious merchandise. 'Pretty good shipment, Uncle Hiram,' he said. 'Canada's finest. How much do you get a case? Or do you peddle it by the quart?'

'Well now,' Uncle Hiram answered, 'does being a college freshman make you an expert on whiskey?'

'I know a smuggling operation when I see it.'

'And I suppose you'll go crying to the police!'

'No, Uncle Hiram. Fact is, I can help you get rid of the stuff.'

I closed the album. Ronald had, in fact, gone in business with Uncle Hiram, selling it on campus, and to the owner of the roadhouse just outside the college town, who became one of his big customers. Nothing was said, of course, to our parents or to Aunt Sarah, but I learned later they all knew that Uncle Hiram was 'importing' various items – whiskey was only one of his lines– but they never knew Ronald was part of the operation until it came to a head seven years ago.

I looked at my watch; it was five past eleven. I decided it was bedtime and went up the stairway from the front hall to my room. There was no sound from Aunt Sarah's or Mrs. Record's room. Aunt Sarah slept over the front parlor; Mrs. Record, across the hall, over the sitting room. My room was next to Mrs. Record's, and the stairs to the third floor started up opposite my door. I couldn't seem to get to sleep; I tried to make my mind blank, but old scenes seethed through it. I lay for over an hour tossing and turning, then the sound slowly impressed itself on me. I sat up in bed. It was a creaking sound – steady, rhythmic, as if someone were creeping up the stairs. I got out of bed and tiptoed to the door. I hesitated a moment, then slowly turned the knob and opened it. The sound was now on the flight to the third floor. I stepped into the hall and looked up. I'd like not to admit what I saw. I'd like to think it was as unsubstantial as the figures my mind had conjured up a few minutes before, for someone was disappearing into the upstairs hall, and the silhouette was unmistakable – the size, the profile, the nose, the hair – Uncle Hiram!

My feet froze on the spot. Then suddenly a voice hissed in my ear.

I whirled.

'See! I was right. It was him!' Aunt Sarah was at my elbow.

I led her back to her bedroom, then went to my own. In spite of the warm summer night, I was shivering. I put on an extra blanket but continued to shiver, sleepless, until dawn.

When I heard Mrs. Record get up, I dressed and went down to breakfast. She looked at me rather sharply, I thought. 'Didn't you sleep well, Mr. Wood?' she asked.

I tried to smile. 'Overtired from the drive, I guess. I had some trouble getting to sleep.'

'Your aunt won't be down for another hour or so, if you'd care to wait.'

'No. I'm afraid I'm the type who has to eat on rising.'

'Me too. We never breakfast together.'

I attempted to sound casual. 'What about this appearance

of Uncle Hiram? Has Aunt Sarah seen him more than once?'

She gave me another penetrating look. 'Why? Do you think she really saw him?'

'Of course not. I just wondered how long she'd had this delusion.'

'It's the only time she's mentioned it. But, you know, the poor dear at times lives in a world of her own. She thought she saw him last night, didn't she? I heard you taking her back to her room.'

'Er-yes. Yes, she did.'

'You didn't see anything, did you?' She stared at me.

I took a big swallow of coffee. 'No. Why? Did you expect me to?'

She laughed. 'Not really. But I've never ruled out the possibility of ghosts. Just wanted to make sure. Not that I'm frightened, you understand. I figure if his ghost is wandering about, it's after the money, not me.'

I'm afraid I started at the knock on the door.

'I guess you didn't get much sleep last night,' was Mrs. Record's remark as she went to answer it. She returned with an athletic-looking young man. 'Agent Herman wanted to see you,' she said. 'I didn't think you'd mind.'

He held out his hand. 'Wally Herman, Federal Bureau of Investigation.' He handed me his credentials.

I asked him to sit down, and before I could offer coffee, Mrs. Record had placed a full cup in front of him. He looked up and smiled.

'Thank you, Mr. Wood,' he said to me, 'I'd like to go over the case with you, if I could. If we don't find something in a couple of days, we're out of it.'

'What do you expect to find?' I asked.

'The money, for one thing,' he said. 'It's got to be around here. It wouldn't walk away by itself.'

'Perhaps it wasn't brought here. Perhaps it was chucked overboard.'

'Unlikely. From all evidence, he carried this through like all his other operations. The government was about to move in on him, anyway, you know. We'd discovered the smuggling ring – the liquor, the jewelry, the furs – quite an operation. The stuff left Canada by boat, was transferred once at sea – very careful, they were – then transferred to the lobster boat and brought in here. When the payroll truck got hit, this was our first stop.'

'Why did you suspect him right off?'

'Well, as you know, the truck was robbed on that lonely coastal road of eight hundred thousand dollars. The guard untied himself, took his blindfold off, and saw two people rowing out and getting on the boat. And, of course, he later identified your brother – his body. It was a hunch at the time, but we just decided to check out Hiram Spinney. They must have had the money on board when they tied up down here because they didn't know then that we were after them. Where did it go?'

'I'm afraid I can't help you.'

'It would help if you'd go over the details of that night,' he said.

'After all these years. I don't know. It's something I've tried to forget, anyway.' I didn't want to go through all that again.

'I wasn't on the case then, you know, but I've read and reread the report. You were very helpful then. I'd appreciate it if you'd help now. I'm here for one last try. Someplace, somewhere, we've overlooked something. I think the answer's here, and I'd like your permission to search.'

'Well, I don't know. This is my aunt's house. I'd have to check with her.'

'You're her legal guardian, Mr. Wood. I'm sure you want to cooperate.'

'Well, if you have to,' I said. 'I don't want to upset my aunt too much.' I thought if he'd get it over with, perhaps he'd leave us alone.

He finished his coffee. 'Why don't we walk down to the shore?' he asked.

I knew then that I shouldn't have come back. I decided I'd leave tomorrow, leave all this behind – for good.

We started down through the field. 'Beautiful day, isn't it?' he said. And it was – clear blue sky with a few puffs of high clouds, warm, the harbor as calm as a lake – so different from the last time.

Herman said, 'It was storming that night, I understand.'

I shivered. I could feel the rain beating on me. 'It was a terrible thunderstorm.'

'We figure,' he said, 'they were going to transfer the money to their other boat and get it to Canada, a sort of reverse of the smuggling line, but the storm came up, and they had to come in. It must have been a job to bring that boat through the storm. I understand it was a bad one.'

'Awful!' I said. 'I never heard the wind howl so, but it didn't cover up Uncle Hiram's shriek as he plunged over the cliff.' I shook my head, trying to lose the sound of the scream, the wind, the thunder, the pelting rain. I still heard it.

'You were visiting here with your parents?'

'Yes. It was the second year that Ronald hadn't come. Dad wanted us to take our vacations at the same time, but Ronald said he was too busy. At the height of the storm, Uncle Hiram, came pounding and roaring at the door, calling for help with the boat. Dad and I grabbed raincoats and followed him down. Then the cars with flashing lights appeared, the men shouting at us and firing shots in the air and Uncle Hiram swearing, and we kept running, for then they were shooting at us. The wind rose, there was an ungodly clap of thunder, and the lightning struck the tallest pine. It fell with a crash, hitting Dad. He never got up. Then Uncle Hiram started shooting at the police. I saw my brother run into the grove, and I chased him. I guess he didn't know me. He started fighting me, savagely. I had to protect myself. Bloody, soaked to the skin, we pounded each other and I knocked him down. His head hit the rock, and I didn't have a twin any more. I started from the trees and saw Uncle Hiram fighting with someone at the edge of the cliff, then I heard that scream as he plunged over the side. The police rushed down the stairs; there was no one on the boat. They secured it as best they could, then found me, collapsed on the platform, when they came back up.'

Herman and I were now at the top of the stairs. The goose pimples stood out on my arms. He said, 'That's just as you had it in the report. Are you sure you've remembered everything?'

'I think I've remembered too much.'

'What was the tide then?'

'High. With the storm, very high.'

He looked down over the side. 'I guess that's why your

uncle didn't hit the rocks. The body was never found.'

'No one could have lived in the water that night. No one!'

'No, probably not. But he was a pretty rugged guy, I understand.'

'He's dead! He couldn't possibly have survived!'

'And this is the grove over here where you fought with your brother? He didn't have anything with him? The money would have been in a steel case.'

I shook my head. I felt as exhausted as I had then. They'd taken me to a hospital, I was there for a week. Both Mother and Aunt Sarah collapsed on hearing the news. Mother never regained consciousness.

Herman was saying, 'If they didn't bring the money up here, and it wasn't on the boat – rather strange, don't you think?'

I shrugged. 'They could have tossed it overboard. It could have fallen over.'

'The area was dragged, but turned up nothing.'

'The seas and a storm can hide many things.'

He said, 'We've looked things over pretty well the past couple of days. Now I'd like to look in the barn and garage. Perhaps Hiram stashed it somewhere before he knocked at the door.'

'Don't you think after all these years . . .' I started to say.

'I don't think your aunt has disturbed much of anything. I'd just like to look if it's all right with you.'

We went back to the house. He gave the garage a casual look, then went to the barn. I didn't go with him. I went into the house.

Mrs. Record told me that Aunt Sarah had seen us down by the water and had refused to get up. She was eating breakfast in bed. I said I would get her tray, and went up to her bedroom.

'What does that man want?' she asked me.

'He's looking for the money, Aunt Sarah.'

'Why don't you tell him where it is, Ronald?'

'Aunt Sarah, look at me.' She looked through and beyond me. 'I'm Don. Donald. Do you understand?'

Her eyes focused on me, and she smiled. 'You can take my tray now. I think I'll get up. Tell that young man I want to talk to him.'

'I don't think that's wise. Besides, I thought you were afraid of him.'

'I just want to see him. Now, bring him into the parlor, and I'll be right down.'

I didn't want to excite her, so I did as I was told. I found Herman in the hayloft of the barn which, for years, had been used for storage.

'Have you been looking around up here?' he asked.

'No,' I said. 'I haven't been in the barn since I got here.'

'Someone's been up here pushing things around.'

I looked away. 'What makes you think that?'

'Dust. Trunks and chests have been moved from where they stood for a long time. Who do you suppose would do that?'

'I have no idea,' I said. 'Aunt Sarah would like to see you. She's waiting for you in the parlor. Please remember she gets quite confused at times.'

He brushed his hands and then his clothes. 'Well, let's go see her.'

As soon as I brought him into the room, Aunt Sarah asked me to leave. They talked for about twenty minutes, as I paced the kitchen, while Mrs. Record prepared lunch.

Herman came out smiling. 'I'll be leaving now. Thanks for your cooperation, Mr. Wood. If you think of anything you want to tell me, I'm at the Seaview Motel.'

I saw him to the door. 'What did she say to you?'

'She just has a theory.'

'She's been mixed up ever since I arrived.'

'She's a nice old lady,' he said, 'but you're right, she is somewhat confused. 'Bye.'

I marched into the front room. 'What did you tell him, Aunt Sarah?'

'Nothing, dear.' She patted my cheek. 'After lunch, you can take Mrs. Record and me over town shopping. We won't have to hire a taxi.'

'Aunt Sarah, did you tell him that you thought you saw Uncle Hiram?'

She looked me right in the eye. 'Of course not. Do you want him to think I'm crazy?'

After eating, we poked around Bellport most of the afternoon. It was very boring for me, and I'm afraid I got impatient. That night, at supper, I told Aunt Sarah that I would be leaving in the morning.

She turned her eyes from me. 'And I suppose you won't be coming back?'

I tried to sound positive. 'Don't be silly, Aunt Sarah. Of course I will.' But I knew she didn't believe me.

Both she and Mrs. Record went to bed early; we couldn't seem to find much to talk about. I went to my room, too, and paced the floor for a couple of hours. I knew what I had to do.

When I felt sure they were both asleep, I packed my things and tiptoed out into the hall. I left my bag by my door and slipped out of my loafers. I knew I had little time, but I wasn't afraid now. Carefully, cautiously, I mounted the stairs to the third floor. There were two doors; I chose the one over Aunt Sarah's room. I could hear snoring behind it. Slowly, I turned the knob and inched the door open. The moonlight poured through the window, over the mattress on the floor and the figure on it. He had aged quite a bit, but he was very much alive – Uncle Hiram. How he ever survived the sea and the storm, and where he'd been these seven years, I don't know. He never got in touch with me. But here he was, obviously back hunting for the money, and resting now, I presumed, for another late night search, perhaps through the barn again. If he'd been awake, I don't know what I'd have done. I closed the door and went back downstairs, put on my shoes, took my bag, and went out the front door. I put the suitcase down by the corner of the house and struck off through the field.

The moon was too bright. I had hoped for a cloudy night, but I didn't have time to be cautious. Besides, no one knew. I was panting when I got to the cliff. The sod, of course, had grown solidly back into the earth, but with frantic digging, I managed to tear it away. Dirt had filled in under the platform, but I found the case and dragged it out. No time to look in it now; I stood up, ready to go.

The hand fell on my shoulder and I froze. I couldn't bear to turn and face him.

'Ah, laddie, so you did hide it. And this time, it's you who'll go over the cliff!'

The voice of Agent Herman interrupted, thank God. 'Mr.

Wood, Mr. Spinney, you are under arrest, charged with robbery and, Mr. Wood, you are charged with the murder of your brother, Donald. You are *Ronald* Wood, aren't you?'

So it ended. They hurried Uncle Hiram off, so we couldn't talk.

Herman said, 'I figure you had the case of money from the boat when you went into the grove.'

I nodded.

'And you and your brother fought, and after you killed him, you decided to change places with him. Then you hid the money here.'

'I just changed the contents of our pockets,' I said. I'd been informed of my rights, but there was no sense in keeping still. It was all over. I knew it. 'Even the people at the bank didn't suspect. When I seemed a bit confused, they were very considerate, knowing what I'd been through. How did you know? You'd never seen us.'

'Your aunt gave me the idea this afternoon. We weren't sure. Just thought we'd watch you. Your Uncle Hiram was an added attraction.'

'But Aunt Sarah's crazy. You know that!'

'I wouldn't be too sure. She was certain Donald didn't like seafood and Ronald did. Even showed me that picture of Donald eating a hamburger at a clambake! And you really enjoyed that lobster last night, didn't you?'

It was another beautiful day as the police drove me out of Bellport and down the coast. If I'd only sensed what was to come; seven years of waiting – for nothing. I should have waited longer. Seven years between trips to Bellport, and both ended in disaster. Now I'd never get back. I looked across the bay to Height Of Land and the house. I thought I saw Aunt Sarah watering her flowers.

The Greatest Robbery on Earth

by Lloyd Biggle, Jr.

The Borgville Bank was held up back in 1937, which was two years before I was born. That might lead you to believe that I don't remember anything about it, and you'd be wrong. Everyone in Borgville remembers the bank robbery. People have been talking about it ever since it happened, and I could describe it just as well as the old timers who actually saw it take place.

Up until yesterday, that bank robbery was the most important thing that ever happened in our town, about the greatest thing on earth. Every state trooper in this corner of the state converged on Borgville. Sheriff Pilkins swore in seventeen deputies, which was only one less than he had yesterday. The mayor wired the governor to call out the national guard. Not only was it an exciting afternoon, but the bank failed a week later because of the robbery, and just about everyone lost some money.

The F.B.I. and the state police were in and out of Borgville for weeks afterwards, and my grandfather was one of the star witnesses. The people in the bank didn't see the robber very well, because he kept his hat down and his coat pulled up over his face. But Grandfather saw him driving away, and he got a good look at him. The F.B.I. took Grandfather away to look at pictures, to see if he could identify the robber. He said he couldn't, and the robber never got caught, and the bank never got its ten thousand dollars back.

It was a nice thing for Grandfather, though. Borgville started to respect him. Grandfather has always been an independent sort of person, and because Borgville is a solid Republican town, Grandfather naturally became a Demo-

that Dav was ideal for the part because, as it happens, I wrote the play. I also know he is happily married, or so it had always seemed, to a lovely girl who had stuck with him during the lean years of role-hunting and summer stock, and with whom he had two children and a home in Fairfield County. I also knew that for the past six months Dav and Patty had been seen together very, very often. I knew that because every columnist in town had reported it at least twice.

I walked up to the bar where Dav was standing alone, and when Eddie looked up I pointed to Dav's glass and said, 'One of those.'

Eddie gave me a look. 'A double Scotch?' He knows I'm a dry sherry man.

Davenport didn't look at all.

'A double Scotch, you Irish mug, and no backtalk.'

Eddie grinned. He insults members all the time, and he gets lonesome if we don't insult him occasionally.

Anyway, Davenport had been sitting, after his matinee yesterday, in Mardi's with Patty Bell, a lady who was once very beautiful and was still an attractive forty-eight. And Howard Bell had walked in.

The morning papers could and did report every detail of what followed because the restaurant was full of Broadway people who knew all three of them. The police had no trouble getting eyewitness accounts.

Dav and Patty had just been served espressos when Bell walked up to their table. He leaned over it and said something to his wife. The other tables could not hear it, and Dav got up and said something equally *sotto voce*. Then Bell pulled a piece of paper from his pocket and threw it on the table, and Dav said something and Bell answered, obviously enraged, and lunged for Dav. Dav pulled a gun.

What followed was as curious as it was sudden. It seems the paper Bell threw down on the table was a note written by his wife. It read: 'Mardi's today the instant after last curtain. The *instant*, dear.'

With it was another note, typewritten and addressed to Bell.

Davenport had rushed to what was their usual meeting place without even changing from the tweed jacket and flannel slacks which were his costume during the third act. He paused only long enough to take a couple of curtain calls, hurried to the dressing room and toweled the make-up off his face, then walked to the restaurant which is around the corner.

Consequently, he carried with him in his jacket pocket the blank cartridge pistol which he uses in the last act of *Next to God* and fires once through an open window at a lurking prowler, as you may recall.

'When Howard came up to the table and started cursing me,' the *Daily News* quoted Dav afterward, 'my only thought was to shut him up. His wife and I are merely good friends, but someone had sent him one of those dirty poison-pen letters accusing Mrs. Bell and myself of all sorts of things, and enclosing this note which told him when and where we were meeting today. He was hysterical – out of his mind.'

In any case, hot and unforgivable words passed between them. Bell, obviously berserk, leaped at Davenport while dozens watched, and Davenport thought of the pistol in his pocket, actually harmless, of course, with its blank cartridges. He pulled it out.

Witnesses agreed Davenport held Bell at bay momentarily with the nickel-plated .32 as waiters began moving forward. Then each man said something to the other, the gun in Davenport's hand drooped down momentarily, and Bell leaped for it. They struggled, each with a hand on the gun. Black coffee spilled over Patty. She screamed. She leaped up, grabbed wildly at both men, and the gun went off – twice. The waiter closed in.

Patty sank forward onto the table, and then slipped to the floor. For a second the restaurant was unbelievingly silent. No once could accept what they had just seen. Patty was dying.

For the gun had not been loaded with blanks, but with real bullets. One had hit her in the mouth, ranging up into the brain, and the other struck in her left breast not far from the heart. She was dead even before two internes arrived on the run from nearby Polyclinic ...

Davenport drained his drink and said, 'Another,' to Eddie

and Eddie poured it fast. Davenport looked at me for the first time.

I said, 'Hi.'

Only his drink, raised in friendly acknowledgment, answered me. His eyes were dark and weary.

I finished my drink and pushed the glass to Eddie for another. I told Davenport, 'Nobody blames you. It was one of those things. Everyone knows how you must feel. But try to realize tragic accidents like this happen, with no one really to blame.'

It was true that nobody blamed him. He and Bell had both been questioned well into the night by the police, but the morning newspapers had reported the unanimous verdict of the medical examiner, the detectives of the Sixteenth Squad and the Homicide Bureau. It was 'accidental death,' the result of a fantastic coincidence. Both Davenport and Bell had been released.

Investigation had, in fact, revealed an astonishing irony. The gun Dav used in the play was always loaded for each performance by the property man. The property man had recently ordered a new supply of blank cartridges, six 50-load packages, and he had unaccountably been delivered one carton containing live ammunition; the police had found it in the prop room. So when Davenport fired the pistol in the final scene that afternoon, he had shot a real bullet. Examination of the theater's brick back wall proved it.

No one had immediately noticed the small hole in the backdrop, any more than the prop man – as he later said voluminously – had noticed the little snub-nosed slugs in the 'blank' cartridges he had used to load the gun. Patty Bell had thus been killed by an impossible accident, coupled with an unexpected confrontation.

Eddie had walked away out of ear shot. I moved closer to Dav and spoke quietly. 'What made you feel you had to kill her, Dav?'

Only the tightening of his nostrils in a perfectly-chiseled nose told me I was right. That was no surprise; I had already deduced the truth. As you have, I'm sure.

Dav said, 'Are you plastered? Or just some kind of nut?'

'Neither. And you're safe. Shall I tell you why you're safe?'

He was studying the back bar.

'There is a weak spot in your story, but the police will never spot it because they don't know Patty like you do. The weak spot is in the letter that Patty sent. Howard Bell got it yesterday in the mail. That was the day of the killing, so it obviously was mailed the day before. But it made the date of your meeting "today," which is the day that Bell got it. And I will bet that the nasty accompanying letter also emphasized that you two would be meeting at Mardi's at that time.

'Which all means that Patty's note in her own handwriting had to be written some time before. And saved. And used at the right time. By whom? It could only have been someone she was much interested in and had been recently meeting. There is only one such person.'

'You're crazy.'

'No, just moderately reasonable, though what I am suggesting is, on the face of it, completely unreasonable. Why should you of all people send her husband a note like that, plus a scurrilous letter that could result only in a public brawl?

'Why would you possibly do such a thing? Even to conceive of it is fantastic. But look at the result. What was the result? Patty was killed.

'Could you have wanted that? Of course not. You were greatly attracted to her. You had often been seen with her. That is your real disguise, and it as why you dared do what you did in front of a restaurant full of witnesses. You murdered her.'

He was protesting no more. He was listening, his head down.

'Make that assumption, crazy as it seems,' I said, 'and everything else fits. Who had a chance backstage to substitute a carton of live ammunition for one of the cartons of blanks that the property man had, so that it would be found later? You did. Who would have a chance to reload the gun with ammo? The prop man had made no mistake about the blanks, although everyone thought he did. You had the chance. Who could make sure, in firing that shot on stage with a loaded gun, that he would not hit anyone? Only the man firing the gun.'

'How do you – why do you think you know so much?'

'Because I know who had a motive for killing her. I know it and you know it, but the police can never learn it. She was an insatiable woman who used up men like cigarettes, and was astonishingly demanding. Which gets back to my original question. What was it that she demanded of you and that you wouldn't give? Marriage?'

The nod was almost imperceptible.

'So I figured. You love your career, and to further it you would go along with the boss's wife to a point. But you also loved your own wife and family. You wouldn't let Patty make you throw away everything that means the most in your life. So being an actor, you figured out a foolproof way of killing her. Stage a public scene. Lure her husband into a quarrel, by note and then by insult across the table. Draw a gun that you presumably could not possibly know was loaded. Let him start a scuffle for it and, because you are younger and stronger, when the gun was pointed right, pull the trigger a couple of times. Who would ever think it was anything but accidental?'

'What *really* tipped you off?'

'I've told you. I knew Patty once – twenty years ago. I was a young and promising playwright then, and I was considered quite handsome, if I may say so. I was also happily married. So I know what Patty can be like. My marriage ended in divorce, you see. She's lucky to have lived as long as she did. No one's turning you in, Dav. Another drink?'

Incident at Mardi's

by Herbert Brean

There weren't very many members in The Players Club bar when Davenport came in that afternoon; he made his entrance to a small audience. Still, it was a fairly dramatic entrance.

He walked across the room to the bar, looking at no one, and ordered a drink from Eddie. But a backgammon game stopped for a full half minute, and at the Players a backgammon game is hard to halt, even momentarily. One of the pool players looked up, saw who had come in, looked down again, missed his shot, and his opponent missed his shot. Neither swore. This is actually unheard of.

Eddie served Davenport his drink and the room returned to normal.

I cannot say what the others thought, but personally I admired Davenport enormously for what he was doing. It took even more courage than anyone knew, anyone, that is, except Davenport – and myself, if I may be permitted.

I put down the afternoon paper I had been reading and strolled toward the bar. Folding the paper away seemed the tactful thing. Its big headline screamed what was in everyone's mind. The previous evening Davenport had killed, or had a hand in killing, a rather prominent woman.

Patty Bell was her name, the wife of the producer of the Broadway dramatic hit in which Davenport was starred. A young and flamboyantly handsome actor, Melvin Davenport had arrived, theatrically speaking, when Bell selected him for the lead in *Next to God*. Some said Davenport got the role because Mrs. Bell liked him. I don't know. I do know

crat. People were a little suspicious of him, until he saw the bank robber and got to be such an important person.

To understand what happened in Borgville yesterday, you have to know just how the town felt about that bank robbery. It happened twenty years ago, but folks have been talking about it ever since, and for the last twenty years Grandfather has been saying maybe twice a week that he'd recognize the man who held up the bank if he ever saw him again. Grandfather never forgets a face.

Grandfather left the house at one o'clock yesterday afternoon and walked up to Borgville's business section, which he always does when it's a nice day. He stopped in at Snubb's Hardware Store and picked up old man Snubbs' morning paper, then went across the street to the bench in front of Jake Palmer's Barber Shop and sat down in the sun to read.

Grandfather is past eighty now, but on him it's hardly noticeable. He was a blacksmith when he was a young fellow, and he's still built like one. He lost all his hair before he was fifty, so of course he never got gray-headed. Except for his liking to sit in the sun for awhile of an afternoon, he's about as spry as I am – spryer, my mother says. His eyes are as sharp as they ever were, and he still never forgets a face.

Nat Barlow was sitting there with Grandfather, in front of the barber shop, and when a stranger drove up and parked, Nat nudged Grandfather, and said, 'Who's that?'

Grandfather looked over the top of his paper and said, 'That's the bank robber,' and went on reading.

Nat grabbed Grandfather's arm and shouted, 'Are you sure?' And Grandfather said, 'Sure I'm sure. I never forget a face.'

Nat jumped up and ran into the barber shop. There were five or six men in there, talking with Jake, and Nat pointed at the stranger and said, 'That's the bank robber!'

The men tore out of the back door of the shop, and Jake pulled down the curtain in the front window and hung up the closed sign and locked the door. And in ten minutes everyone in Borgville knew that the bank robber had come back.

*

I was over at Borgville Pharmacy having a chocolate malted
and talking with Mollie Adams who was doing this and that
back of the counter. I'd been dating Mollie – I hadn't had a
chance, yet, to find out how emotionally unstable she was –
and someone called in through the back door that the bank
robber was back in town and coming our way.

Mollie and I were still staring at each other when the
stranger walked in. He was a nattily dressed, trim-looking
man well past middle-age. There were streaks of gray in his
hair, and the bags under his eyes had been there longer than
overnight. He looked as if he'd been really handsome once,
and he acted as if he thought he still was. He winked at
Mollie, and said, 'Hi, girlie, got any cigarettes?'

Mollie had a lemon-meringue pie on the counter that she'd
just started cutting, and she picked it up and threw it at the
stranger. He must've been five, six feet from her, but it
smacked him squarely in the face, and Mollie ran out the
back door and stood in the alley screaming.

The stranger grabbed some paper napkins from the
counter and started wiping pie off his face and clothing. I'd
like to tell you what he said but I won't. You don't hear that
kind of language very often in Borgville, and I probably
wouldn't get it right.

He cleaned himself off some and walked out. Next door to
the pharmacy is the Borgville Garage. The service entrance
was open, and the stranger saw a cigarette machine near the
door. He walked in and started fumbling in his pocket for
change.

Bob Adams was there, working on my jalopy, and of
course someone had told him that the bank robber was in
town. Bob didn't ask questions. He just threw the wrench he
had in his hand. It wasn't such a good idea, because the
wrench was heavy and Bob's hand was greasy. The wrench
didn't go anywhere near the stranger. It broke the windshield
on Doc Beyers' new Cadillac. As for Bob, he crawled under
my jalopy and stayed there until all the excitement was over.

The stranger ducked out of the garage and walked on
down the street to the Star Restaurant. Old Mr. Gregory was
standing behind the counter, near the cash register. When he
saw the stranger, he ducked down and crawled away on his
hands and knees. And when the stranger walked up and

looked over the counter, there wasn't anyone there.

Things were happening all over Borgville. Mr. Hanson, the bank president, sent his teller down in the basement and hung the *Bank Closed* – Legal Holiday sign on the door, and locked it. He locked the time vault and the back door too. Then he found a sack of money in the teller's cage that the teller had forgotten to put in the vault. He was running in circles trying to figure out what to do when Fred Dimmit came down the alley to the back door with a bag full of money.

Fred had dumped all of his grocery store money into the bag, and he brought it down to the bank, because the bank's money was insured and his wasn't. He pounded on the back door, and shouted, 'Let me in! I want to make a deposit!' Mr. Hanson shouted back at him, 'The bank is closed!' They were still pounding and shouting at each other when the state police got there.

Sheriff Pilkins was one of the first to hear about the bank robber coming back, and the sheriff prides himself on being a pretty smart man. He said to himself, Why try to capture him uptown and destroy a lot of property, and maybe get some people shot? Why not set up a road block and capture him when he tries to leave?

The sheriff radioed a call to the state police, and then he collected a lot of shotguns and swore in as many deputies as he could find, and went out to the south end of town to set up a road block. Joe Hammer happened to come along in his tractor, pulling a trailer load of corn to the Farm Bureau, and the sheriff stopped him, and upset the trailer across the road, and blocked off one shoulder with the tractor. That still left the other shoulder, so the sheriff stopped Mike Wilkins and told him to put his Model T there. Mike's Model T didn't have much in the way of brakes, and so it slipped down into the ditch. Mike claims that now his Model T doesn't run the way it did before and he's threatening to sue the sheriff.

The stranger didn't know anything about this, of course. He came out of the Star Restaurant and hurried back up Main Street towards his car. People were peeking out of windows and doors watching him, but Grandfather was the only person in sight. He was still sitting in front of the barber

shop, reading the paper. The stranger walked up and started
to talk to him.

Just then Mrs. Pobloch, who lives up above the barber
shop, stuck her husband's shotgun out of the window and
pulled the trigger. She said afterwards she wasn't trying to hit
anything; she just wanted to scare the man away. She did
that, all right. The blast went across the street and broke the
window of Snubbs' Hardware Store, and the stranger tore
back to his car and drove off.

Unfortunately for Sheriff Pilkins, the stranger drove out
of town to the north, so the sheriff's road block didn't do any
good. The only thing it accomplished was to make the
state police waste quite a bit of time at the south edge of
town, while they waited for the sheriff to get Joe Hammer's
trailer off the road. The sheriff said later that in the
excitement he was thinking that the North Road still dead-
ended on Manning's pasture.

As soon as the stranger left, a mob of people hurried out to
crowd around Grandfather, which made him plenty mad.
He said it was a fine thing when a man couldn't sit in the sun
and read the paper without folks standing around staring at
him. Everyone wanted to know what the stranger had said,
and Grandfather told them, 'He asked me if everybody in
this town is nuts, and I asked him what he expected from a
town full of Republicans.'

That was all we could get out of Grandfather. When the
state police finally got there and asked him about the bank
robber, Grandfather said, 'What bank robber?' They kept on
asking him questions until he got disgusted and went home.

Things were kind of mixed up after that. People stood
around arguing about what kind of a car the stranger had,
and what color it was, and what he looked like. The only
ones who'd gotten a close look at him, other than
Grandfather, were Mollie and I. Mollie was too hysterical to
remember anything, and I decided to play dumb. I said that
the only time I saw him he had pie on his face, so of course I
wouldn't recognize him.

I guess the state police would have agreed with the
stranger about everyone in Borgville being nuts, if it hadn't
been for Mr. Snubbs and Jeff Morgan. When Mr. Snubbs
heard that the bank robber was back, he peeked out the door

of his hardware store and wrote down the stranger's license number. And Jeff Morgan, who sinks just about every penny he gets ahold of into photographic stuff, went up to his sister's apartment above the bank with his camera and one of these telescope things, and got half a dozen good shots of the stranger walking down Main Street.

Most of us didn't know anything about that. And after the state police left, folks went back to whatever they'd been doing, and by the time the reporters got there Borgville had more or less decided to forget about the whole thing. The reporters had a tough time finding anyone who would answer questions.

I followed Grandfather home, and found him sitting on the front porch. He was acting grumpy, but I thought that was because he hadn't gotten to finish his paper while the sun was right.

'What was all the excitement about?' Grandfather said.

'You should know,' I told him. 'For the last twenty years you've been saying you'd recognize that bank robber if you ever saw him again, and naturally people got upset when you said he was back.'

'Oh,' Grandfather said. '*That* bank robber.'

'What bank robber did you think it was?'

The only answer I got was a couple of grunts, so I went in the house. Five minutes later Nat Barlow came along. He started shouting when he was still half a block away. 'Lookee here, Bill Rastin, you know darned well you told me that fellow was the bank robber!'

Grandfather didn't say anything, and Nat stormed up on the porch and stood there with his fists clenched. Nat's a frail old man, and if Grandfather had come up with a good, loud sneeze it would have knocked him over.

'What fellow?' Grandfather said.

'Why, that fellow who – who –'

Grandfather picked up the paper, and opened it up to an inside page in that lordly way he has when he's riled up about something. 'Look,' he said. 'See that picture? Bank robber, it says. This fellow robbed a bank down in Mississippi, it says. You *can* read, can't you? I was reading the paper. Right here, I was reading, and you said, "Who's that?" and I said, "That's the bank robber." Now take a good look. Isn't it the bank robber? Read this. Doesn't it say he's the bank robber?'

Nat stared at that picture for maybe two minutes, and then he turned around and stomped down the porch steps. He went around the house and out the back gate and sneaked home down the alley, realizing whose fault it really was.

Grandfather threw down the paper and went upstairs to his room. As soon as his door closed, I tore out on the porch to get that paper. I took a good look at the picture of the bank robber, and then I went upstairs to see Grandfather. He was sitting in the rocking chair in the corner of his room, smoking his corn cob. Usually he rocks about sixty per, but this time he was just sitting there.

'Gramps, there's something funny here,' I said. 'This paper – it's today's paper, but pages three and four and nine and ten are dated two weeks ago.'

Grandfather took the paper and squinted at it. He looked confused, which for him is definitely normal. 'Yeah,' he said. 'Just like them city slickers to try to peddle their old papers in Borgville. Snubbs ought to get his money back.'

'I'll tell him about it,' I said. I tucked the paper under my arm, and started for the door.

'Say, Chuck,' Grandfather said. 'I wouldn't bother Snubbs about this. As long as he didn't notice it ...'

'Okay,' I said. 'I won't say anything.'

I stood outside his door for a moment, waiting for the rocking chair to start up, but it didn't.

If you've read today's papers, you know how the state police caught up with the stranger a hundred miles upstate, and how they chased him for miles and finally cornered him at a road block, and how they found he was one Walter Donaldson that the F.B.I. had been wanting for a bank robbery that took place a month ago over in Illinois. That was quite a confession they got out of him, and of course one of the things he mentioned was that he'd robbed the Borgville Bank twenty years ago, and he'd gone back to Borgville to look the place over and see if he could do it again.

The reporters started coming before we were out of bed this morning, and they kept coming. They filled the living room, and I went up half a dozen times to try and get

Grandfather to come down to talk to them. He was still sitting in his rocking chair, looking as if he'd been there all night, and I couldn't make him budge. And when one of the reporters sneaked around to the kitchen door and went up the back stairway, Grandfather told him the stranger hadn't looked anything like the man that robbed the Borgville Bank. When he tried to ask some more questions, Grandfather threw two pairs of shoes at him.

That reporter was plenty mad, but he quieted down when I told him Grandfather was just being modest – about recognizing the stranger.

Quite a few people from Borgville had dropped in by then, excited about the state police catching the bank robber. The reporters got the whole story – about how Grandfather had been the only person to get a good look at the bank robber twenty years ago, and how he kept saying for twenty years that he'd know him if he ever saw him again, and how he'd recognized the stranger the minute he drove up and told Nat Barlow that there was the bank robber. Nat was there too, grinning and nodding his head, and the reporters seemed to think it was a pretty good story. I dug up a snapshot of Grandfather and took the negative over to Jeff Morgan, and he made prints for all the reporters.

When I got home, Mom was sitting in the kitchen, worrying because Grandfather hadn't come down to breakfast. He wouldn't come down to lunch, either, though he ate what I took up to him. And when I took him the afternoon papers to show him the big story and his picture on page one, and how they were saying he might get a reward, he shoved me out of his bedroom and threw the papers out after me.

'What's the matter with him?' I said to Mom. 'He ought to be proud of himself. *I'm* proud of him.'

Mom looked sad, and a little worried. 'I think I finally understand, Chuck,' she said. 'And I've decided it'd be best if we don't say anything more about this. You see, this man Donaldson was a relatively young fellow when he robbed the bank. Dad recognized him the second he saw him yesterday, but when he got a closer look at him it probably shocked him to see how old he looked. Dad hasn't seemed to notice that the people he sees every day are getting older, and he can't understand how that young bank robber now can be a man well up in his fifties. He doesn't want to admit that that's possible, and it's worrying him terribly. He's started thinking about how old he's getting himself.'

'All right,' I said. 'I won't mention it again.' And I thought I wouldn't ever say anything either about that old newspaper Grandfather got, that had the picture of the bank robber in it.

I went out and sat down on the porch, and for the first time in my life I felt sorry for Gramps. Because I understood what he was doing up there, sitting in his rocking chair and not rocking.

He was looking in the bureau mirror.

Damon and Pythias and Delilah Brown

by Rufus King

Within this subtropical dreamland of alcoholic divorcees, in this bar-studded playground of the suspicious rich, in this Florida of sunshine, palm trees, nag and dogtracks, bars, jai alai, bolita, bookies, bars, surf-swept beaches, a moon, and bars, lived a young married lady with the first name of Delilah, her surname being Brown.

It happened that Delilah Brown was one of those special young women who crop up every now and again like Cleopatra or Circe or Pompadour or Gypsy Rose Lee, and who drive otherwise sensible men straight out of their wits.

In a case like hers mere looks do not matter, although Delilah had plenty, such as titian hair, deep-sea eyes, good bones and good bumps to go with them. It is the inner woman that counts, that certain ferrous quality, always in a state of magnetic flux, that can draw a man with even the trace of a nail in his head right into a condition of animal, mineral, and vegetable collapse.

The hunting ground through which Delilah scalped when off duty from her job as hostess in Grandmother Katy's Kitchen was the seaboard town of Halcyon, a homelike little community somewhat to the north of Miami. Apart from its seasonal glut of shrimp pink tourists, the place is inhabited largely by retired yankees, disillusioned motel owners, heat-baked construction workers, somewhat larcenous bar operators and an assortment of deep down Southern crackers.

(Word lore note: the term cracker in its Southern sense has nothing to do with a barrel or Nabisco. It derives from the early Florida settlers' prima donna habit of cracking their whips over the flanks of their oxen, mules, or horseflesh – and sharp-eared little Susie, as a consequence, saying to her pea-shelling mother, 'Hark, Ma, here comes a cracker,' and Mother understanding her perfectly.)

Well, Delilah was a cracker and her husband Pythias Brown was a cracker and Pythias' construction-boss-and-best-friend Damon Lang was one too.

Although the boys' friendship was on a common plateau of unshatterable fondness, the economic stature of Pythias and Damon were far apart. The Langs had prospered abundantly through several generations of turpentine stands, citrus groves, and eventually valuable real estate, leaving the resultant boodle in Damon Lang's husky, well-molded hands – a provocative situation which more than frequently caused Delilah Brown to think, think turgidly.

If (she would turgidly think) I were married to Damon instead of to Pythias, I would have that kidney-bean-shaped swimming pool, that Jaguar and that 65-foot dream yacht, and I would have unlimited charge accounts at Burdines and at Jordan Marsh, instead of an installment rating at Sears Roebuck and a credit card with Texaco.

Damon, per se, never clearly entered the picture because men to Delilah were simply men – handy rungs on a ladder to an ultimate Monaco or an Aga Khan.

Now Delilah was not the type of girl who sits idly by and lets her dreams remain dreams. When she positively decided she wanted something she would put her well adjusted thinking cap on her titian hairdo and sort out all practical approaches to her goal. The basic solution to her immediate dream-compulsion was, naturally, for Pythias to be evaporated into outer space and for her ensuing state of pathetic widowhood to be rectified posthaste by a marriage with good, dependable, protective, and filthy rich Damon Lang.

What had sparked this lethal thought process into activity was the irritating announcement by Damon of his engagement to a svelte snowbird, a Miss Ethel Chalice, whose Westchester family wintered in Fort Lauderdale. Miss Chalice was generally considered by Delilah's coterie to fall loosely within the category of a female meat-head, due to her absurd interest in puppet shows, ceramics, ballet, Aldous Huxley, and kindred paranoiac subjects.

Delilah was not alarmed, she was simply spurred from a contemplative jog trot into a gallop. She was personally satisfied that the Chalice nuisance was little more than a resigned move on Damon's part of accepting second-best. He was definitely the marrying male, and as pal Pythias had removed his one true passion (herself) from the market, a sensible ceremony with the Winchester drip was his best out. The wedding was scheduled for December, leaving Delilah a comfortable margin of three months for arranging her husband's encore act to the Sputniks.

How?

Suffocation? Blunt force? Gunshot? Ice pick? Rat poison? Delilah considered them all, judicially chasing their drawbacks about in her clever young head while she seated and soothed and politely kidded the stuffed customers in Grandmother Katy's Kitchen, or as she glowed magnetically while drowning several cool ones at a neighborhood tavern, or especially while she and Pythias were involved in the (to her) shopworn gestures of love after the two-o'clock curfew had eased them away from the taps.

It took about three weeks of speculative prospecting before she hit pay dirt, in what satisfied Delilah as a recipe for the perfect crime. Reasonably simple, enchantingly original – this it was – and leaving her grief-shocked self triumphantly in the clear.

All she needed was a goat.

Delilah pin-pointed this goat in the bulging, perspiration-moistened person of a Dr. Hillegas Dow. Dr. Dow was also a cracker – in fact, everyone concerned in this simple pastiche on homicide was a cracker except for the sheriff's deputy and the B.C.I. man who were shortly to be slapped with the case in the middle of a sopping wet and windy night. And, of course, the peripheral Ethel Chalice.

Delilah knew Dr. Hillegas Dow both inside and out, being on liquid terms of gossiping intimacy with a Mabel Oestringer who held down the job of nurse-receptionist at Dr. Dow's small clinic. Delilah knew him to be licensed in chiropody and as a naturopath, facts that apparently barred him from practicing in any of the hospitals, and that he had

had to establish his private clinic in order to cash in. She was further happy in the conjecture that his professional ethics were as flaccid as a dying girdle and that his one-and-only god was the fast buck.

Definitely, Dr. Dow appeared not to be what even his kindest colleague would call a dedicated man. He was reputed to be far more interested in the pattings and pinchings of the comely than in therapeutically patting the ill. He was undoubtedly one of the exceptions to the rule that can be found in any line of professional work.

During a pre-dawn hour of the Wednesday-Thursday night of October 16th, while Pythias breathed deeply in guileless sleep, Delilah explored the pockets of his slacks and then arranged the first ingredient of her recipe for wishing him a bon voyage. Needless to say, it was not three cups of sifted flour.

The weather forecast for Halcyon and vicinity (said the 6 o'clcok A.M. newscaster) *calls for fair skies and mild temperatures today and Friday* ...

'Nuts,' said Delilah, snapping off the radio set and getting back into bed.

'What did you say, sugar?' Pythias asked drowsily.

'I said nuts.'

'Why?'

'Because the man said clear weather.'

'Good. Damon and I have that job to inspect over on Bricknel.'

'You got about one hour more sleep coming. Turn over and take it.'

'Friday:

The weather forecast for Halcyon and vicinity calls for partly cloudly skies today with occasional showers late tonight and Saturday ...

'And just why only occasional?' Delilah said irritably, snapping off the set and getting back into bed.

Sunday:

The weather forecast for Halcyon and vicinity calls for cloudy skies and increasing showers over the weeked ...

'That's better,' said Delilah.

Sunday.

... A low-pressure area in the Caribbean will cause an

increase in the rainfall both today and Monday. Motorists are advised to exercise special caution while ...

'Now that's my boy,' said Delilah, getting back into bed and landing a solid punch on the back of Pythias' solid neck to wake him up.

'How – when – what's the idea, sugar?'

'Do you know what day it is tomorrow?'

'Yes.'

'Well, what?'

'Monday. Look, Del, this is the one morning in the week when I can sleep –'

'What else day is it besides Monday?'

'Damon and I got that Harrison job to look over.'

'And is that all that Monday October the twenty-first means to you?'

'Isn't it enough?'

'Wake up and listen to me, you bleak catfish. Monday is my birthday.'

'Why?'

'*Why?*'

'Sure, why. Last year it was in November. Come to think of it, the year before last it was June.'

'So this year it's tomorrow.'

'Del, honey, if it's that leopard-spotted velvet stole you're thinking about at Japeson's –'

'I am thinking about no leopard-spotted velvet stole at Japeson's or at any other cut-rate trap. I am thinking that tomorrow is my day off from Grandmother Katy's kind home for old mice, and that I want you and Damon to give me my yearly birthday party irregardless of the date.'

'Okay, sugar. How about knocking it off now so I can get some sleep?'

'I want both you and Damon to take me for a charcoal broil at Tropical Joe's. Damon is marrying that pixy potroast-special in six or seven weeks, and this may be our last good party like old times. Just the three of us all alone together. Just Damon, just you, and just me.'

'Look, babe, don't choke it to death. I said yes. I'll give him a buzz, if I can for one more time get back to sleep again.'

And so with the few medical facts Delilah had gleaned

from Mabel Oestringer, along with the rather less than flattering portraiture of Dr. Hillegas Dow, and with one pertinent bit of information she had casually lifted from Damon, and with the time now set for the launching, the deadly casserole was ready for the oven. Hot. 375 degrees.

'Wella, wella, well,' said Tropical Joe with his celebrated originality as he watched Damon and Pythias and Delilah steer a homing-pigeon course from the wet doorway to the wet bar, 'if it isn't the Three Muscatels.'

Delilah smiled magnetically back at Joe's greeting and automatically counted the house: ten parboiled tourists, three deadpan crackers with their lady friends, and one stupefied ex-jockey with an Amazon lush. Not at all bad for a storm-flooded Monday night.

She herded her mutually devoted escorts through some sets of martinis (Pythias), manhattans (Damon), old-fashioneds (herself) and then over to a table for charcoal-broiled steaks and beer.

The long established pattern of their threesome get-togethers held, with Pythias and Damon absorbed in construction business chitchat, and Delilah occupied in stoking away the groceries and in exchanging the eye with any mobile individual in pants.

Several hours and a good many squat ones later, Delilah rang the departure bell. The pattern continued to hold. As usual, she drove. As usual, Pythias lapsed into a state of negligible consciousness on the seat between herself and the painlessly un-consolidated Damon.

Windshield wipers battled against a tropical downpour that blurred road visibility through a sheeting of water, and Delilah held the speed down to twenty-five while glissading over slick blacktop until, vague in the distance, a chaste neon sign announced the clinic of Dr. Hillegas Dow.

It was a lonesome span of road, made melancholy on one side by scrub palmettos and on the other by a hyacinth-choked canal. She had scouted the route several times before tonight, and knew exactly the location of a tall Gru-gru palm tree with its thorn-spiked trunk and large top of feather leaves that stood close by the entrance drive of the clinic.

Perfectly cool in her head, despite a warm lower down

flush from the evening's liquid potpourri, Delilah swept a
mental eye across this moment in which the show was to
start. Her devoted consorts were both ripe for a good night's
sleep with their eyelids already comfortably composed, a
single-edged safety razor blade was ready in her bag, and the
rain-lashed highway fore and aft was empty of traffic.

She took a skipper's look at the looming Gru-gru palm
tree, depressed the accelerator, swung the wheel, braced
herself, and muttered, 'Gold Coast, here I come!'

The effects were reasonably spectacular. Pythias and
Damon lunged in unison against the windshield, to their
somewhat detriment, splintering it.

Delilah, having prepared herself against compact, suffered
little beyond a momentary loss of breath. Swiftly, she took
the single-edged razor blade from her bag. Swiftly, she used
it. Then she jumped out onto the clinic driveway and started
a crescendo of screams.

They were agreeably effective. Dr. Hillegas Dow emerged
from the clinic and ran towards the screamer. He was
followed by his nurse-receptionist, Miss Mabel Oestringer.
By the time they reached the wrecked car, Damon had
sufficiently recovered from shock to struggle out and take
some befuddled steps over to Delilah, who adjusted herself
about him warmly.

Delilah went into her act. It was important that she
establish her concern for Pythias, and even though her gears
remained enmeshed with Damon, she cried desperately to
Dr. Dow, 'Help Pythias! He's still in the car! He may be
bleeding to death!'

It is interesting to note that Damon promptly dropped
Delilah like a hot potato, even while her physical contact was
shooting through him with bolts of fire. He lunged for the
car. And even though both young men were of equal tonnage
and size, Damon managed under the press of anxiety to
extricate Pythias and to carry him on a trot towards the
clinic, crying 'Snap into it, Doc! He's bleeding like a stuck
pig.'

Dr. Dow snapped. What had initially struck him as being
nothing more than an interesting motor accident was now
translated into a source of cash, in what had been an
otherwise cashless evening. First aid, he decided, then at

least a week of expensive recuperation in the clinic.

'Shall I phone for an ambulance?' Mabel Oestringer suggested as she trotted beside him.

'Certainly not!' And Dr. Dow added, as a conscience-quieting clincher, 'The man would be dead before an ambulance could possibly get here.'

This made little sense to Mabel, but then little ever did beyond the delicious properties of vodka and her weekly take home pay of $42.60.

Throughout this group-trot along the driveway, Delilah did not lose her impressario touch. She aligned herself beside Damon and established her loyalty as a wife by hysterically saying into Damon's closer ear, 'If Pythias dies I'll kill myself. It was all because I didn't control the skid. And I'd rather end it all than go on living with the horrible thought.'

It worked to an extent, for Damon called time out from his deep anxiety over Pythias, fleetingly, to admire Delilah's noble self-recrimination and noble anguish.

'Forget it, Del,' he snapped soothingly, while hustling on with his bleeding-to-death burden. 'That road was pure vaseline. Even a bulldozer could skid on a night like this.'

Within the clinic's antiseptic walls, the command post fell to Dr. Dow, and in all truth the doctor was neither a complete dud nor a quack.

He directed Damon to place Pythias on a surgical table, and was disturbingly aware that the situation was critical. Obviously, Pythias had lost and was losing a dangerous amount of blood from a wrist slash that had severed an artery. Odd, Dr. Dow thought abstractedly as he went about compressing the flow.

Odd, in the sense of the wound's location. The minor head and face lacerations were understandable, but unless Pythias had struck out in some witless moment of thrashing, and a shard of windshield glass had sliced the artery ...

'He must have an immediate transfusion – and I mean immediate.'

'I'll give it,' Damon said, adding with earnest selflessness, 'He can have my last drop.'

'Have you ever donated, Mr. Lang? Do you know your type?'

'Yes. Type A.'

'You absolutely sure?'

Damon took out his wallet and leafed through its plastic compartments.

'Here, Doc. Take a look.'

'Oh, stop quibbling and give it to him!' Delilah cried. 'His poor, dear skin looks like a slice of boiled liver.' Her agitated voice rose higher still. 'Give him blood!'

'Miss Oestringer–'

'Yes, Doctor?'

'Please take Mrs. Brown into the waiting room and keep her there. Perhaps one of the yellow capsules.'

'Yes, Doctor.'

The clinic's waiting room was principally a matter of chairs, ash-tray stands, and Mabel Oestringer's desk. Mabel shook out a barbiturate.

'Want this, hon, or a slug?'

'Both,' Delilah said.

Mabel produced vodka.

'Join you,' she said, doing so, and then dialing the telephone.

'Who are you calling?'

'Sheriff's office.'

'Why?' Delilah's voice held an edge.

'Well, somebody has got to, hon,' Mabel said reasonably. 'Anytime now, a patrol car will maybe spot the mix-up heap and will then ask why it was not reported and we'll be in a snit – oh, hello? Sheriff's office? Chuck? Well listen, honey boy, this is Mabel and ...'

Some twenty minutes later honey boy blew in, with his fullback body creating the effect of a minor atmospheric disturbance in the quiet room.

'Chuck, I want you should meet Mrs. Delilah Brown,' Mabel said.

Chuck did so and suffered the usual male reaction upon first facing Delilah, of having been blasted by a pleasing booby trap. This over, he said to Mabel, 'Bill is down investigating the wreck. What gives in here?'

'Bill?' Mabel looked puzzled. 'Isn't Bill B.C.I.?'

'He is. Happens Bill was in the office and losing his shirt at stud. He just came along for the ride. And now, ma'am, Mrs. Brown? Could I have just what happened?'

But Dr. Dow appeared and broke in upon Delilah's Sarah Bernhart interpretation of the dramatic night. Dr. Dow was both bewildered and a badly shaken man.

He said, 'he's dead.'

It is fantastic how swiftly during a moment of absorbing triumph, disaster can strike and the tired old cliché about the cup that slips on its journey to the lip can get in its deadly licks.

Never had Delilah so richly enjoyed the sweet and pitless fruits of success. Beneath her Academy performance of just-widowed grief, she was one utterly satisfied and contented cat. She had even managed to radiate through her quiet sobbing a few hot shafts at Bill, the Bureau of Criminal Identification man, who had finished with his examination of the wreck and for the past twenty minutes had been closeted with Chuck and Dr. Dow in the room where Pythias was lying in the long sleep.

Twenty minutes?

Remotely, the length of time – for what after all should have been a simple look-see – was beginning to overlap Delilah's mood of total security. The thought seeped through her complacency: there is danger in that man. Something he knows. But how could he? And what? She worked on the problem, while Damon's worthy right arm circled and comforted her port side and Mabel bolstered up the starboard.

'I feel so lost – so alone,' she sobbed.

'You've got me, Del,' Damon said. 'You've always got me.'

'And me,' Mabel said.

'Thank you, both of you,' Delilah sobbed simply, while in her coldly calculating thoughts the questions continued: What does that man know? From the wreck? From what is taking place in that room in there right now?

The razor blade?

Scarcely. She had tossed it into the shrubbery, and on a storm-lashed night such as this ...

'Pythias was my very best friend,' Damon was saying in a voice charged with restrained emotion. 'And you were everything to him, Del. It is my aim and duty to shelter you as Pythias would shelter you, if – if he were still –'

Damon's honest baritone voice broke, and Delilah was

engaged in the twin thoughts of how perfectly Damon was reacting according to plan and how silly were her unreasonable doubts when that B.C.I. man came back into the room with a purposeful strid˄.

Bill carried his six foot two inches of whipcord intelligence and superlative B.C.I. training over to the trio.

'With your permission, Mrs. Brown?' he said.

Without waiting for the permission but just taking it for granted, Bill lifted Delilah's bag from her lap and clumped out its contents onto the receptionist desk. His manner was so quietly assured, so officially confident of being within his legal rights (which he wasn't, and knew it) that the trio of competent young adults watching him were momentarily changed into hypnotically transfixed children.

He was about to pick up the wallet from among the trivia in Delilah's bag when his attention was caught by a small cardboard guard. He held it up carefully by its edges.

'You find these shields on new single-edged safety razor blades,' he said.

Bill set it to one side back on the desk.

'The blade itself will be looked for,' he said, 'in the shrubbery near the wreck, after sunup.'

'Damon, sugar,' Delilah sobbed (she was still at it), snuggling closer with Damon's arm, 'what is the man talking about? Make him stop.'

'Something in the nature of a razor blade was used to cut an artery in your husband's left wrist, Mrs. Brown,' Bill said. 'The location and nature of the wound rules out the probability of its coming from windshield glass.'

Delilah froze into a cold, clear-thinking cube of ice.

'It *was* the windshield glass that made my dear, dead husband bleed. And what is more,' she added, to restore the situation clinchingly back where it belonged, 'I screamed my head off getting him help so that Dr. Dow could see to it that he got an immediate transfusion and his life be saved. Why should I move both heaven and earth to save him if I had been so foolishly cruel-hearted as to want him to bleed to death?'

'It was the transfusion that killed him,' Bill said. 'It was the transfusion that was *meant* to kill him, Mrs. Brown.'

'Don't say that!' Damon cried in horror, releasing Delilah

for the second time that evening like a hot potato. 'My blood
– no, not *the blood I gave*–'

'Yes, Mr. Lang. It was your blood that killed him. Wrong
type. Mr. Brown died from cardiac and cerebral embolism
due to your blood corpuscles collecting into clumps. Dr.
Dow recognized the symptoms during the transfusion, when
he had got over his shock and thought back about it – skin
turning blue – rapid pulse – labored breathing – death –
happens most likely when the donor's blood is type AB and
the recipient's type is O. Cases on record about it.'

'But Pythias's blood was type AB too. Same as mine,'
Damon said, drifting deeper into the horror of it all.

'No, his blood group was type O. Dr. Dow has just
finished testing it.'

'Dr. Dow don't know his blood-testing, or any other kind
of testing, from horse feathers,' Delilah insisted inelegantly.
'My husband's type was AB. It's marked right on his driver's
license.'

Bill selected Delilah's license from its cellophane folder in
her wallet.

He studied with satisfaction the small box in its lower
right-hand corner labeled BLOOD TYPE. A space provided
on licenses by the State of Florida, for the operator to print
in his own blood group, for swift use in case of an
automobile accident when an instant transfusion would be
required.

'I see that your type is B, Mrs. Brown. Did you print it in
yourself?'

'I did and what of it?'

'Just that our handwriting expert will testify it matched
the B you added to your husband's license – after you had
changed the original O into an A by drawing a line down on
either side of it and straightening its curved bottom into a
crossbar. Like they change the cattle brands out west.
Showed up plain under Dr. Dow's miscroscope, Mrs.
Brown.'

Bill added – as Damon groaned in tortured horror, and as
Mabel plunged for the vodka, and as Delilah changed into a
shrieking female – 'Weirdest murder weapon I ever came
across in my life.'

Glory Hunter

by Richard M. Ellis

When the buzzer buzzed at the front entrance, Homer Doyle set down his mug of lukewarm tea – he never drank coffee after midnight – and rose from his chair behind the desk. He crossed the lobby to the heavy glass door and clucked disapprovingly at the young man smiling in at him. He released the latch and pushed the door open a few inches.

'I thought my sister might have turned up,' the young man said eagerly. 'I know it's late, but –'

'Almost three o'clock in the morning,' Homer Doyle said with some asperity. 'Your sister isn't here. Perhaps she went to some other hotel.'

The young man's sandy brows puckered in a frown. 'No. She was definitely supposed to come straight here from the airport. I don't understand it.'

'She might have met someone on the plane –'

'Oh, no. Betty isn't that kind of girl,' the young man said, looking a bit shocked.

Doyle grunted dubiously. He had been night-clerking at the Cragmore, a small hotel for women, more than long enough to decide that almost any girl was that kind of girl. He said, 'Well, I'm sorry, she just hasn't shown up. No one has checked in since you were here earlier.'

He started to pull the door shut.

'Could I come in long enough to use the phone?' the young man asked. He gestured to the dark, deserted street stretching into the hot summer night on either side of the Cragmore's lighted entrance. 'There doesn't seem to be another place open along here. I want to call the – the police. I really am worried about Betty.'

Homer Doyle hesitated.

The Cragmore was run very much like the nearby YWCA; no male visitors were allowed inside the building after midnight, when the front door was locked. 'Propriety' and 'Cragmore' were synonymous.

Doyle nodded. After all, the boy was obviously only concerned with locating his sister, and there was a phone booth just inside the lobby.

Inside, the young man waited while Doyle shut and locked the door. The rather large lobby was in shadow; the only lights on were Doyle's reading lamp behind the registration desk, and the tiny yellow bulb above the elevator.

'Certainly different from when I was here before,' the young man said. 'The place was swarming with girls then.'

Doyle nodded vaguely. The boy had come in around ten or ten-thirty last night, inquiring for his sister who had supposedly arrived in the city earlier in the evening.

Perhaps she had, but she hadn't checked in at the Cragmore. The young man, who had given his name as Bob Ed Lambeth, had hung around for several minutes with a sort of polite but dogged persistence until Doyle had gone through the registration cards twice with the same result. Finally, after a long look around the then busy lobby, the young man had left.

Now Doyle said, 'The phone's over there. I suppose you've checked to make sure your sister's plane arrived on schedule last night?'

'What? Oh, yes.' Lambeth fumbled in a pocket of his sports jacket. 'I think I'll need change.'

Doyle sighed and turned toward the desk. He took two steps, and then his head suddenly exploded in a great burst of white light followed by a shower of sparks that died into nothingness.

He woke to find himself in his familiar chair behind the registration desk, but with a most unfamiliar pain throbbing in his head. He groaned and tried to lift his hands. He couldn't move. He blinked dazedly up into the concerned face of the young man who had wanted to use the phone.

'Thank goodness,' Lambeth said. 'I was afraid I'd hit you too hard, Mr. Doyle.'

'What –'

'Would you like a drink of water?'

Doyle shook his head, winced, and again tried to lift his hands. Then he saw that his arms were bound securely to the arms of the chair, with some kind of heavy cord that also encircled his chest, holding him firmly against the back of the chair.

Lambeth was saying, 'I'm sorry I had to slug you but I couldn't be sure you weren't carrying a gun or something. I had to play it safe.'

'Gun?' Doyle said dazedly.

'After all, you are down here on the ground floor alone, and there's no house detective or anyone like that in the hotel; just you and the manager, Mrs. McVey, and of course she's fast asleep in her room up on the top floor.'

Along with the throbbing in his head Doyle began to feel anger, most of it directed at himself. This kid with his guileless air and fresh-scrubbed face had taken Doyle in completely.

Doyle swore under his breath. Then he glanced toward the small safe set into the wall behind the desk. The safe had been closed, but not locked; now its door was ajar.

Doyle snapped, 'I see you've cleaned out the cash box. I hope the fifty bucks you found in there is enough, because that's all there is.'

Lambeth didn't appear convinced. 'I don't –'

'Of course, I might have all of five dollars in my wallet,' Doyle added bitterly.

'Six, as a matter of fact,' said Lambeth, with a deprecating smile. 'I searched you while you were unconscious. I also found a gun in this little drawer under the counter here. I'll just take that along ... But I'm really not interested in money, or guns. This is what I was looking for.' From the desk he picked up four sheets of stiff paper, floor plans of the hotel, one for each of the four upper floors. Small removable tags indicated which rooms were occupied and which were not.

Doyle stared.

Lambeth said lightly. 'No, I'm not still trying to find my sister. Actually, I imagine Betty's sound asleep at this hour, in her own bed at home. Way out in Seattle, Washington.

She really did stay here once, though, when she came east on a visit. She told me all about this place. Thought it was very nice. Very quiet and respectable.'

Doyle frowned uncertainly at the young man. He noticed that in spite of Lambeth's casual chatter and outwardly calm manner, there was a sheen of perspiration on his face, and his hands were trembling. 'You've got all the cash in the place,' Doyle said. 'Why are you hanging around?'

'It's not quite three-thirty yet,' said Lambeth, nodding toward the wall clock. 'There's nothing to do but wait.'

'Wait for what?'

Lambeth made an abrupt gesture. 'Do you like this job?'

'Now, listen –'

'It sounds like it would be – interesting. Night clerk in a hotel for women, one man alone with all these girls. I'll bet you could write a best-selling book about your experiences, huh? Even at your age, it must be interesting.'

'Are you kidding?'

Lambeth shrugged, his pale gaze again flicking to the clock. He took off his jacket and folded it neatly over a corner of the desk.

He said, absently, 'I suppose if you were the lecherous type, you wouldn't have this job in the first place. Not in a respectable place like this is supposed to be ... Well, it's almost time. I'll just –'

'Time for what?' Doyle cried. 'What the hell is all this?'

As he spoke, Doyle struggled against the cord that bound him to the chair and discovered that there was a certain amount of give in the loops encircling his left arm and the arm of the chair on that side. He immediately stopped his efforts; Lambeth didn't seem to notice.

Lambeth was busy. He had taken off his shirt, and Doyle saw that the young man's naked, hairless chest was covered with curious designs done in greasepaint; jagged streaks of red and green radiating from a bright yellow spiral.

Now Lambeth took a tiny mirror and a stick of yellow greasepaint from his trousers pockets and carefully drew crude stars on his cleanshaven cheeks and a sunburst on his forehead.

Doyle watched, his eyes bulging.

'Just an added touch,' Lambeth said, with an embarrassed

grimace. 'It's the kind of thing that goes over big in the newspapers.'

'Sure. Uh-huh,' said Doyle soothingly. Until now he had been more annoyed at his own gullibility than afraid of Lambeth. The kid was hardly the type to inspire terror, but if he was a psycho, that was something else again.

Lambeth eyed the clock. 'Three-thirty. Good. That's the time my father died, some years ago. Three-thirty on a hot summer morning ... He died of acute alcoholism, Mr. Doyle. Driven to it by my mother. How does that grab you?'

Doyle tried to moisten his dry lips with a tongue that felt like parched leather. 'I – I'm sorry –'

Lambeth burst out laughing. 'Don't be. Just between us, my old man died of a coronary, but the other way sounds much more interesting.'

'Sure.'

'Well, to work,' Lambeth said briskly. 'I've looked at these floor plans. I believe the top floor is best. I see there are seventeen guests on that floor, most of them in single rooms. That'll make it easier, you know.'

'What are you –'

'See, I can go quietly from room to room, using this master key I found in the safe. With just one girl to deal with in each room – except in a couple of cases where there are two – there won't be any unnecessary uproar or bother.'

Doyle shook his aching head. He wondered if he might be having some kind of weird hallucination; but the pain was real enough, and so was the needle-pointed ice pick that Lambeth had taken from a sheath attached to his belt.

Doyle sat there, frozen, while the young man tucked the chart of the top floor under one bare arm and with a casual nod walked around the end of the desk and started across the lobby. He was humming softly.

'Wait,' Doyle croaked. 'Listen, you can't mean –'

'Sure I do,' Lambeth said, his face shining with sweat and greasepaint. 'What the heck, I'll soon be twenty-four, and who's ever heard of Robert Edward Lambeth? Nobody. But in a few hours, Mr. Doyle – in a few hours I'll be the most famous man in the country – in the world.'

'But –'

'I'll be down as soon as possible. Then I'll untie you, and

we can call the television stations and the newspapers – and the cops, I suppose.' Lambeth grimaced. 'Don't worry about a thing, Mr. Doyle. After all, you'll be the man who took my surrender. Wish me luck.'

Lambeth reached the elevator and slid open the door. He stepped inside and, with a last cheerful nod, punched the button and the door slid shut.

Whimpering, Doyle strained and tugged at the cord; almost at once his left arm was free.

'My God,' he panted. 'Seventeen – he'll kill ...'

Now his right arm was free, and only the cumbersome loops of cord around his chest held him in the chair. If he could free himself before the elevator reached the top floor, there was an emergency switch that would override the controls inside the elevator itself, stopping it between floors. If Doyle could just reach that switch in time ...

He glared across the dim lobby at the indicator above the elevator door. The hand of the indicator was moving slowly past 2 and on toward 3.

Doyle tried to stand up but he was still entangled in the stiff new cord. He groaned.

That psycho would kill those women, one by one, entering their rooms and stabbing them with that ice pick before they knew what was happening, and Doyle had no doubts remaining that Lambeth meant to do just that. Seventeen ...

It would be the most horrible crime ...

Lambeth would be famous, all right. Oh, yes!

At last Doyle was able to stand up partially, his eyes glued to the elevator indicator; it had reached 3, and there was only 4 – and then 5, the top floor.

There was still time, though. The switch was on a panel in an alcove behind the desk, only a few steps from where Doyle was struggling to push the last loop of the cord down past his hips so that he could step out of it.

Famous? Lambeth would be more than famous. There would be hours of television about him, miles of newsprint devoted to him, magazine articles, books– if Homer Doyle didn't stop him in the next few seconds.

And what about the man who caught Lambeth? Right now it would mean nothing. But afterwards, after seventeen murders ... That man would be almost as famous as Lambeth!

Doyle stood there in a sudden blinding agony of indecision.

Then, slowly, he sank back into the chair. He stared in fascination at the elevator indicator. Then he slowly pulled the last loop of the cord back up around his waist.

After all, not only the young have dreams of glory.

Perfectly Timed Plot

by E. X. Ferrars

Rina Evitt's eyes were stretched wide with fear. Staring across the room at her husband, they were not quite focused.

'It'll never work,' she said shrilly. 'Never.'

'It'll have to.' Harry Evitt's voice was as empty of feeling as hers was charged with it. His nervousness was in his feet. With one heel, he was trying to kick a hole in the costly gray rug before the fire. 'Yes, it'll have to,' he said without excitement, without doubt, without eagerness.

Rina dropped her head into her hands. Her hair tumbled over them as her fingers clawed her bursting temples. She had thick, bleached hair, with a sheen that was bright but lifeless. Her face was long, with slackly handsome features and big, wide-spaced eyes.

'I'll make a mess of it – there isn't time – there's too much to remember.'

Knowing what she could do when she tried, her husband was not much troubled.

'You'll remember, all right,' he said. 'It's just the timing that matters. The rest's easy. But make sure you get the timing right.'

He shifted his weight from one foot to the other, dug the back of one heel into a new patch of the rug and gave a fierce twist to his foot.

'You've got to be sure the others leave on time,' he said. 'And you've got to be sure you get Minnie out into the drive with them, to see them off, so that you can come back in here and change the clock and make that telephone call without her knowing. And you've got to time that exactly. But the rest of it's easy.'

Rina jerked her head up, staring at him again.

He was a man of middle height, softly covered in flesh, dressed in a dark gray suit, a white shirt, a dark blue tie, all good, all inconspicuous. He had a round, white face, moulded into insignificant features, and had thinning dark hair brushed back from a low curved forehead.

With her eyes on that calm, dull face, Rina said, 'You haven't just thought of all this, Harry – not just today. You've had it ready for a long time, in case George ever found out about the money. You have, haven't you?'

'All right, I've had it ready,' Evitt said. 'And a good thing I did, I'd say.'

'You've had it all ready, yet you never told me ...'

'You know that's what I'm like,' he said. 'You ought to be used to it by now.'

She swayed her head from side to side, not quite shaking it, not quite nodding. Crouched in her chair, shrunk into herself, she looked small, helpless and harmless. In fact, she was a tall woman, thin, but big-boned and strong. But her apprehension had dwarfed her.

'I'm not used to it,' she said, 'I never shall be.'

Evitt's pale pink lips twitched at the corners in a faint expression of satisfaction. But life never remained long in his face.

'Remember – get them all out into the drive,' he said, coaching her again with patience, with understanding, but with relentlessness. 'Then run in and change the clock and make the telephone call. Make sure Minnie stays outside long enough for you to do that. Get her worrying about the roses. Or fertilizers. Anything. You can handle her.'

'But the other part of it,' Rina said, 'suppose *that* doesn't work. Suppose –'

'It will.'

'No, it's too difficult. It's too complicated. There are too many things to go wrong.' Her voice had leapt again into shrillness.

After a short silence, Evitt answered evenly. 'All right then, what do we do instead?'

When she did not answer, he said, 'Go and get changed now, Rina. Put on your green dress. Get the room ready. There isn't much time to spare.'

She looked round dazedly. 'The room's all right, isn't it? Just as usual.'

'The room's fine.' His pride in the room escaped into his voice for a moment.

It was a room of which they were both proud. The floor was of mahogany woodblocks. The picture window showed them a sweep of lawn, some early daffodils blooming in rough grass under bare trees, distant roofs and still more distant hills, the tranquil English countryside. The antique furniture had been bought after careful study of the best magazines. There was central heating.

'The tea's all ready,' Rina added. 'I've just got to get out the bridgetable and the cards.'

'Get them out then,' Evitt said. 'Keep busy. Don't sit and think. It won't help you.'

'And you ... ?'

He walked over to her. He put his hands under her elbows and with slow deliberation hauled her up out of her chair.

'Don't think about me either, my dear.'

She was slightly the taller of them, even without her high heels. Face to face with him now, she could look over his head to the window, to the cluster of leafless trees and the gray-green line of the low hills beyond them.

'You can do it, Rina,' he said, his hands tight on her arms. 'I am certain of it.'

'I suppose I can do it,' she said. 'But I don't like it.'

'Do you think I like it?'

He did not like it. He was terrified of what he had to do and of what might result from it for himself and for Rina. He was a calculating rather than a violent man. But calculations can go very easily wrong, and then what is there left but violence?

Rina's bridge-party broke up at six o'clock. It always did. Two of the four women who met every Wednesday to play had to catch a bus home from the end of the road at ten minutes past six. So when the hands of the grandfather clock in the corner pointed to ten minutes to six, the losers groped in their handbags, paid out shillings and pence to the winners, re-hashed the blunders and disasters of the last rubber and made peace with each other. It was a scene which repeated itself week after week.

'Not my lucky afternoon,' Minnie Hobday said in a tone of unusual heaviness. She smoothed back one of her straying locks of gray hair, but left several others, disturbed by the high wind of play, to droop around her square, mild face and support its gentle, sheepdog quality. 'I'm getting too old for this game.'

Rina, sitting on her left, scribbling on a scoring-pad before her, tapped Minnie on the wrist with her pencil, a gesture that Rina seemed to be fond of. The pencil was of emerald green, tipped with gilt, and matched the emerald green woolen dress and the heavy gold bracelet of intricate design that she was wearing.

'It isn't age that's the trouble,' she said, smiling. 'You've got something on your mind, Minnie. Isn't that so?'

'No, it's age,' Minnie Hobday said insistently. 'I never had much of a memory for cards, and soon I suppose, in just a few years, I shan't have any at all.'

The truth was, however, that she had a great deal on her mind, that she was very worried, because for the last three days her husband George had barely spoken to her, and today he had gone to London without telling her the reason, all of which was decidedly quite unlike him.

But even if Minnie had reached the stage of wanting to confide in someone the terrible suspicion that had been torturing her all day, the suspicion that George was not well, that he had symptoms so fearful that he had not been able to bring himself to tell her about them, but had gone off alone to London to consult a specialist, it would never have occurred to her to confide in Rina Evitt. Though the two women had never had a quarrel, and during the five years since Rina's marriage to George's partner in the firm of Hobday and Hobday, auctioneers and estate agents, had made a habit of these weekly bridge afternoons, and of performing all sorts of small neighborly acts for one another, Minnie had never even begun to grow intimate with the younger woman.

She was sorry for this. It would have been far better for all of them if she and Rina had been able to become as friendly

as George was with Harry. But Rina, so Minnie, blaming
herself, explained it, was young, was smart, had travelled,
and apparently, in other places, had known really interesting
people. So she could hardly be expected, could she, to be
anything but bored by Minnie Hobday?

Minnie had always been aware of the boredom in Rina, of
the emptiness, of the need for something more than she had.
And it was Minnie's belief that it would always be for more
and more. Whatever Rina had would never be enough. Still,
it had been clever of Rina to realize that she had something
on her mind. Ordinarily, she seemed so wrapped up in
herself, so like a child in a daydream, that you would no
more expect her to notice a shade of worry on an elderly face
than, come to think of it, you would expect her, all of a
sudden, to be interested in the names of two undistinguished
shrubs, growing near the gate, and which had been growing
there for years.

So perhaps something was happening in Rina, some
change, some development. That would be nice, Minnie
thought, walking out to the gate with the other two women,
and identifying the shrubs as a laurustinus and a hypericum
uralum. But turning to Rina to tell her this, Minnie found
that she had just turned back into the house, and this
surprised her somewhat.

Minnie did not leave then, for George had said that he
would call for her on his way home from the station, and
Rina was expecting her to wait for him. Returning to the
house, Minnie found Rina setting a tray with a decanter and
four glasses on it on the low, tile-topped coffee-table.

'I didn't see why we should wait for the men,' Rina said. 'A
drink is what you need to cheer you up a bit. I suppose it's
Michael you're worrying about, but you shouldn't, you
know. He's all right, that boy. I'm fond of him.'

Michael was the Hobdays' son, and because of a certain
carelessness that he had sometimes shown in the handling of
a fast car, he had more than once given his parents cause to
worry about him. But recently he had been almost sensible.

'No, I'm not worried about Michael,' Minnie said. 'Really,
I'm not worried about anything.' She took the glass that
Rina held out to her and glanced at the clock. George should
be here at any moment, she thought; the suspense of the long

day, thank heavens, would soon be over.

However, it was not as late as she had thought that it must be, or so she believed until, a minute or two later, she happened to glance at her watch.

In surprise, she exclaimed, 'That clock's wrong, Rina!'

'Not *that* clock,' Rina said emphatically.

'It is, it's ten minutes slow,' Minnie said. 'George ought to be here.'

Rina shook her head. There was a smile in her wide-spaced candid eyes. 'It's the most reliable thing on earth, Minnie, and so it should be, considering what care Harry takes of it – and what he paid for it.'

'But this watch of mine is quite reliable too. I've had it for twenty-two years, and I never had to adjust it more than about two minutes in a month.' Because of her worry, Minnie sounded querulous. 'It's a very good watch. And the thing is, it always has been.'

Rina turned to the fire. She stirred the smoldering logs with the toe of her shoe. Her pale hair, swinging forward, hid her face and its tense expression.

'Perhaps it needs cleaning,' she said.

'I had it cleaned two months ago. No, I'm sure it's the clock that's wrong. George ought to be here ...' The sound of strain in her voice checked Minnie.

'All right,' Rina said equably. 'I'll tell Harry. But talking of Michael, he's a crazy thing, but really so nice. Everyone thinks so. And even if he and George do cross one another, at times, you shouldn't make up your mind it's all Michael's fault.'

Frowning vaguely, Minnie wondered why Rina kept dragging Michael in. 'I don't know what you mean about him and George crossing one another,' she said. 'They're ever such good friends nowadays. Of course, Michael went through a difficult time. All boys do.' She stopped, because she thought that she had heard footsteps outside on the gravel.

Rina had heard them too. 'There's Harry,' she said.

'Or George.' Relying on her watch rather than on the Evitts' clock, Minnie believed that her husband's train must have reached the station about ten minutes ago, and she knew that by the short cut across the fields, he needed only five minutes to reach the Evitts' house.

'Yes – or George,' Rina said, and with long strides went quickly out of the room.

Nervous and impatient, thinking of the dire news that George might be bringing her, Minnie made one of her random selections of an untidy lock of hair and smoothed it back from her forehead. At the same time she did her best to arrange a placid smile on her face. But it was Harry Evitt, not George, who received the smile.

'Ah, Minnie!' he said with pleasure.

'Good evening, Harry,' she said. 'You haven't seen George, I suppose? He was going to call in for me.'

Evitt looked at the clock.

'Wasn't he coming on the six-twenty? That's only just due now.'

'But that clock's slow,' Minnie said. 'It's half past six.'

'*That* clock isn't slow,' Evitt said, almost as Rina had said before him.

In a shriller voice, as if it mattered which was wrong, the Evitts' clock or her watch, Minnie said, 'Well, by my watch it's half past six already. George ought to be here. He said he was going to come straight here and not go to the office.'

The Evitts exchanged puzzled glances.

'Well, let's check it on the telephone,' Harry Evitt said. 'You may be quite right, Minnie. If you are, I expect it's just that the train's late, but if you like, I'll walk to the station and just make sure ... make sure ...' He stopped, as if he were uncertain of precisely what, in the circumstances, he ought to make sure.

Rina had already gone to the telephone. She picked it up, spoke into it and put it down again.

'The operator says it's six-twenty-one by the clock in the exchange,' she said, and picking up the glass of sherry that she had left behind when she had gone out to meet her husband, she drank it down and began to choke.

Evitt hit her between the shoulders. The sound his hand made, striking her, was surprisingly loud and hollow-sounding.

Wiping moisture from her eyes, Rina said hoarsely, 'It's really Michael Minnie's worried about. That row they had.'

'That was nothing,' Evitt said. 'Nothing at all. Have some

more sherry, Minnie. George'll soon be here.'

But even an hour later, George had not as yet arrived at the Evitts' house.

The Evitts said that he must be coming on a later train. Minnie agreed with them, and decided not to wait for him any longer. Evitt saw her down the short lane to her home. He went with her as far as her gate, then walked off into the darkness, while Minnie walked up the path to the door, a door set in a jutting Victorian porch, that opened into a roomy but drably papered hall, across which an electric clock faced her, noisily whirring. Comparing her watch with the clock, she saw that her watch was fast, but only by three minutes.

That was at seven-forty.

At seven-fifty-five the police arrived. George had not come home by a later train. He had returned from London, as he had said that he would, on the six-twenty, the ticket-collector quite clearly remembering his handing in his ticket. Then George had started to walk across the fields, directly to the Evitts' house.

At the time when his body was discovered, under a hedge and with his head battered in, he had been dead for at least an hour.

Detective Inspector Ronald Tewson was very interested in Minnie's watch. Had she or had she not re-set it at the Evitts' when she found that it and their clock did not agree? But Minnie by then was not in a state to give him an answer on which he could place much reliance.

In grief, at first, she had maintained a dreadful, vacant composure. She had told the police all that she could, but had grown quietly more dazed and incoherent, till her son Michael, a tall boy of nineteen, who had been summoned home from a cinema, had led her upstairs to her room and the doctor had given her an injection that made it possible for her to rest.

As he watched her go, not losing her gentle restraint, but only her mind, Tewson, who could almost deceive himself that he could take murder in his stride, felt something in himself that he dreaded, the sense of pressure, caused, as he knew, by extreme anger. For this, he was certain already, was a cold-blooded crime, and of all kinds of crime, that was the kind that made his own blood hottest. But with that anger in him, he always wore himself out, suffered more than was useful to anyone, and jumped to unwarranted conclusions. The unwarranted conclusion to which he jumped before that night's work was over was that George Hobday had been murdered by his partner, Harry Evitt. All that funny business about the clock and the telephone call to the exchange ... It was too convenient. But Tewson was not going to have anyone else saying anything of that sort yet.

'We haven't a thing against Evitt at the moment,' he said dourly to Sergeant James Geary, at one o'clock in the morning, as the two men gulped tea in Tewson's office. 'That's the fact. Not a solid thing except that Mrs. Hobday doesn't think she reset her watch before she got home. Doesn't *think* so!' He shook his head despairingly. 'A solid fact, d'you call that?'

Geary was a younger, heartier man than Tewson.

'Look,' he said, 'it's the telephone call that's the only trouble, isn't it? The fact that they've confirmed it at the exchange that Mrs. Evitt did ring up and ask the time at six-twenty-one – which made the Evitts' clock right and Mrs. Hobday's watch wrong, and put Evitt right here in the room with Mrs. Hobday when Hobday's train got in, and for an hour afterwards. That's all that worrying you, isn't it?'

Tewson nodded his head, in furious parody of a definite nod of agreement.

'Of course a little thing like motive doesn't worry me,' he said, his lips drawn back in a tight, ugly smile.

'You'll find that in the books of the company, I shouldn't wonder,' Geary said. 'There's been talk around for some time, about where Evitt was getting his money from. When you've talked to that accountant Hobday went to see in London ...'

'Go on and teach me my job,' Tewson said. 'It's that telephone call you're going to put me right on, isn't it?'

'There were two telephone calls,' Geary said.

'That's right,' Tewson said, 'there probably were. One to the exchange and one to nowhere, and the one Mrs. Hobday heard was the one to nowhere. It could have been like that. Only if it was, I don't like it.'

Geary was disappointed that his thinking had already been done for him.

'Why not?' he asked. 'It's nice and simple.'

'Simple!' Tewson said, as if the mere sound of the word made him ill.

'Look,' Geary said, 'they arrive for the bridge-party – Mrs. Hobday and the two other women – and they play for a couple of hours. All three have got watches, but not one of them says anything then about the clock being slow. And the party breaks up at the usual time, because two of them have to catch a bus. And they all go out in the garden together to see the two ladies off, and Mrs. Hobday also goes to look at some shrubs, because Mrs. Evitt suddenly got interested in knowing what they are. But for some reason, instead of going with Mrs. Hobday to look at the shrubs, Mrs. Evitt doubles back into the house, and when Mrs. Hobday follows her, she's setting out drinks in the living room. But by then Mrs. Evitt had three or four minutes to herself, and that would be plenty to ring up the exchange, get told that the time was six-twenty-one, then put the hands of the clock back to six-ten. Well then, presently Evitt comes in. It's really six-thirty, and he's met Hobday at the station, started across the fields with him, done him in and gone on home. But the clock says it's only six-twenty, and when Mrs. Hobday says the clock's wrong, they make a fake call to the exchange which convinces the old lady for the time being that her watch is wrong. Now tell me what's the matter with that?'

'Only that her watch wasn't wrong when she got home,' Tewson said, 'or only three minutes wrong, which doesn't signify. Or –' he rubbed the side of his jaw thoughtfully '– or I should say doesn't seem to.'

'But it's her watch not being wrong that proves all this,' Geary said.

Tewson gave a weary shake of his head. 'Evitt – a man like Evitt – he'd have thought of that, Jim. But when we saw him, he wasn't scared. Things had worked out just as he meant them to. So he's got something else up his sleeve, and that means there's something else coming, something for us to trip over and send us flat on our faces. Yes ...' Tewson stopped as the telephone rang at his elbow, then, as he reached for it, repeated somberly, 'Yes, something else is coming.'

His conversation on the telephone lasted for some minutes. When it was over, he looked expressionlessly at Geary, then leaned back in his chair, stared up at the dingy ceiling and muttered, 'Didn't I say something else was coming?'

'What was it?' Geary asked.

'That was young Hobday,' Tewson said, 'His mother's watch is now thirty-five minutes fast. In about six hours, it's gained nearly half an hour. What do you make of that, Jim?'

In disgust, Geary exclaimed, 'That means her watch *was* wrong at the Evitts'. She must have re-set it there and forgotten doing it. And it had already gained another three minutes by the time she got home. It's hopelessly out of order. Or did anyone get a chance to tamper with the watch?'

'The boy says not. He says she talked to him quite sensibly for a little while when he got her alone before the injection hit her, and she was quite sure no one had a chance to tamper with it.'

'Then you aren't going to be able to swash Evitt's alibi so easily, are you?'

'Because of the sheer coincidence that her watch, her good watch, that she's had for twenty-two years, went wrong the same evening as her husband was murdered?' Still staring at the ceiling, onto which, at one time or another, he had projected most of his problems, Tewson shook his head. 'No,' he said definitely.

'Then someone did tamper with it – stands to reason someone did,' Geary said.

'Yes.'

'The boy?'

'Why?'

'Working with Evitt, perhaps. There's this story that he was on bad terms with his father.'

'The Evitts' story. No one else supports it.'

'But then ...' Geary found himself staring at the ceiling. But he was unable to draw from it the inspiration that Tewson seemed to find there. Once more he fixed his eyes on Tewson's face, which at that moment was almost as gray, as lined and as blank as the ceiling which he was able to put to such good use.

'But then no one but Mrs. Hobday could have tampered with the watch,' Geary said. 'Mrs. Hobday herself. Only why should she do it? She seemed fond of her old man. So why should she do that to protect Evitt?'

'Just let me think, Jim,' Tewson answered. 'Just let me think.'

In the morning, Harry Evitt did not go to the office. He knew that this was a mistake, but he was afraid to leave Rina by herself. The day before she had done her part well. Both in the handling of Minnie Hobday and of the police, she had shown the nerve and resourcefulness which he had known would be roused in her by excitement and the presence of an audience. But in the morning, after a night quite without sleep, alone in the house, she was not to be trusted.

He knew that she ought to go round to the Hobday's house to inquire after Minnie, but he doubted if he could make her go. She clung to him, needing to be continually reassured that all had gone as he had planned. So when, in the middle of the morning, the police reappeared, Evitt felt from the start at a disadvantage. He felt that he must explain his own presence at home, when surely, of all times, he was needed at the office, and that he must apologize for Rina's failure to be the kind, concerned friend of the bereaved woman that would have seemed only natural under the circumstances.

'My wife's so upset, Inspector ... A bad night ... Perhaps a prowler around somewhere ... Afraid ... You understand ...'

The words limped out uncertainly. They weren't the right words, Evitt knew, even as he produced them. A murderer should never explain or apologize.

What made it worse was that, for all the notice that Tewson seemed to take, Evitt might not have spoken at all. Tewson had followed him into the living room, had nodded briefly to Rina, who had risen from her chair by the fireplace, then he had stood glancing around the room with the air of looking for something. The fact that he had the air of knowing just what he was looking for made Evitt's plump hands turn to ice.

He crossed to Rina's side. Standing on the gray hearth-rug with his shoulder touching hers, he reached automatically for the warmth of the fire. But yesterday's wood fire, for decorative purposes only in the well-heated room, was a heap of ashes.

'I came to tell you,' Tewson said, 'that Mrs. Hobday has withdrawn the statement she made to us yesterday evening that your clock was wrong. She believes now it was her watch that was wrong. Since it was practically speaking right when she reached home, she suspected you at first of having altered your clock and lied to her about your call to the exchange, in order to create a false alibi for yourself. But she now believes she must have unthinkingly re-set her watch while she was here.'

Tewson had been looking at the grandfather clock while he was speaking, but now his eyes rested on Evitt's face.

Evitt gave a grave nod, almost a bow. He was striving to assume a solemnity of sorrow for his dead friend and partner. It made a certain slowness of utterance, while he chose his words, seem understandable. But it was difficult to keep his feet still.

'I see,' he said. 'May I ask what made her change her opinion?'

'Her watch went on gaining after she got home,' Tewson said.

'Ah, I see. Just an unfortunate coincidence, then.'

'Was it?' Tewson gave a tightlipped, ferocious smile. Then he moved away. He crossed to the telephone and stood looking down at it. 'That's what she herself believes it was. An unfortunate coincidence. But I'm not sure ...' He had picked up a little writing-pad from beside the telephone, the kind of pad intended for the jotting down of messages. From across the room its cover had looked as if it were of tooled leather, of emerald green and gold. But in fact it was of painted metal, cold to the touch of his fingers. 'I'm not sure that I agree with her. Mrs. Evitt, what did you do with the pencil that belongs to this pad?'

Rina started. Evitt could feel the trembling begin in the arm that was pressed against his. But her voice was only a very little higher than usual. No one who did not know her well would have noticed it. With an audience to play to, he thought, you could always rely on her.

'The pencil?' she said. 'Why, I – I don't know. Isn't it there?'

'I mean the pencil,' Tewson said, 'a green and gold pencil, with which, as Mrs. Hobday told me this morning, you kept tapping her wrist yesterday afternoon, her left wrist, all the time you were playing bridge – tapping her watch too pretty often, of course.'

'Did I do that?' Rina asked. 'I don't remember. Oh, but you don't mean that *that* could have upset her watch?'

Evitt took it up quickly. 'No, Inspector, surely you aren't suggesting that you can deliberately make a watch go wrong – because I take it that that's what this might imply – by giving it gentle little taps with an ordinary pencil?'

'Not with an ordinary pencil, no,' Tewson said. 'That isn't what I'm suggesting. But I know these pads. The pencils that go with them have magnets in them. That's to make them hold onto the metal covers of the pads, the idea being that you won't mislay them. Neat, if you can be bothered with that sort of thing. And if you keep on tapping a watch with a quite powerful magnet, you can make it go very wrong indeed. You can't tell *how* wrong, of course. You can't tell if it'll go fast or slow or stop altogether. All you can be pretty sure of is that with that magnet drawing at the works, they're going to be badly enough upset to make the watch useless as evidence against a fine old clock like that and a faked call to a telephone exchange. Now where *is* that pencil, Mrs. Evitt?'

There was silence in the room. For a moment the Evitts stood close to one another, both tense, wary and wooden-faced. Then Rina drew away from her husband, clawed suddenly at his round, empty face with her nails and started to scream at him.

#8

by Jack Ritchie

I was doing about eighty, but the long flat road made it feel only that fast.

The red-headed kid's eyes were bright and a little wild as he listened to the car radio. When the news bulletin was over, he turned down the volume.

He wiped the side of his mouth with his hand. 'So far they found seven of his victims.'

I nodded. 'I was listening.' I took one hand off the wheel and rubbed the back of my neck, trying to work out some of the tightness.

He watched me and his grin was half-sly. 'You nervous about something?'

My eyes flicked in his direction. 'No. Why should I be?'

The kid kept smiling. 'The police got all the roads blocked for fifty miles around Edmonton.'

'I heard that too.'

The kid almost giggled. 'He's too smart for them.'

I glanced at the zipper bag he held on his lap. 'Going far?'

He shrugged. 'I don't know.'

The kid was a little shorter than average and he had a slight build. He looked about seventeen, but he was the baby-face type and could have been five years older.

He rubbed his palms on his slacks. 'Did you ever wonder what made him do it?'

I kept my eyes on the road. 'No.'

He licked his lips. 'Maybe he got pushed too far. All his life somebody always pushed him. Somebody was always there to tell him what to do and what not to do. He got pushed once too often.'

The kid stared ahead. 'He exploded. A guy can take just so much. Then something's got to give.'

I eased my foot on the accelerator.

He looked at me. 'What are you slowing down for?'

'Low on gas' I said. 'The station ahead is the first I've seen in the last forty miles. It might be another forty before I see another.'

I turned off the road and pulled to a stop next to the three pumps. An elderly man came around to the driver's side of the car.

'Fill the tank,' I said. 'And check the oil.'

The kid studied the gas station. It was a small building, the only structure in the ocean of wheat fields. The windows were grimy with dust.

I could just make out a wall phone inside.

The kid jiggled one foot. 'That old man takes a long time. I don't like waiting.' He watched him lift the hood to check the oil. 'Why does anybody that old want to live? He'd be better off dead.'

I lit a cigarette. 'He wouldn't agree with you.'

The kid's eyes went back to the filling station. He grinned. 'There's a phone in there. You want to call anybody?'

I exhaled a puff of cigarette smoke. 'No.'

When the old man came back with my change, the kid leaned toward the window. 'You got a radio, mister?'

The old man shook his head. 'No. I like things quiet.'

The kid grinned. 'You got the right idea, mister. When things are quiet you live longer.'

Out on the road, I brought the speed back up to eighty.

The kid was quiet for a while, and then he said, 'It took guts to kill seven people. Did you ever hold a gun in your hand?'

'I guess almost everybody has.'

His teeth showed through twitching lips. 'Did you ever point it at anybody?'

I glanced at him.

His eyes were bright. 'It's good to have people afraid of you,' he said. 'You're not short any more when you got a gun.'

'No,' I said. 'You're not a runt any more.'

He flushed slightly.

'You're the tallest man in the world,' I said. 'As long as nobody else has a gun too.'

'It takes a lot of guts to kill,' the kid said again. 'Most people don't know that.'

'One of those killed was a boy of five,' I said. 'You got anything to say about that?'

He licked his lips.

'It could have been an accident.'

I shook my head. 'Nobody's going to think that.'

His eyes seemed uncertain for a moment. 'Why do you think he'd kill a kid?'

I shrugged. 'That would be hard to say. He killed one person and then another and then another. Maybe after awhile it didn't make any difference to him what they were. Men, women, or children. They were all the same.'

The kid nodded. 'You can develop a taste for killing. It's not too hard. After the first few, it doesn't matter. You get to like it.'

He was silent for another five minutes. 'They'll never get him. He's too smart for that.'

I took my eyes off the road for a few moments. 'How do you figure that? The whole country's looking for him. Everybody knows what he looks like.'

The kid lifted both his thin shoulders. 'Maybe he doesn't care. He did what he had to do. People will know he's a big man now.'

We covered a mile without a word and then he shifted in his seat. 'You heard his description over the radio?'

'Sure,' I said. 'For the last week.'

He looked at me curiously. 'And you weren't afraid to pick me up?'

'No.'

His smile was still sly. 'You got nerves of steel?'

I shook my head. 'No. I can be scared when I have to, all right.'

He kept his eyes on me. 'I fit the description perfectly.'

'That's right.'

The road stretched ahead of us and on both sides there was nothing but the flat plain. Not a house. Not a tree.

The kid giggled. 'I look just like the killer. Everybody's scared of me. I like that.'

'I hope you had fun,' I said.

'I been picked up by the cops three times on this road in the last two days. I get as much publicity as the killer.'

'I know,' I said. 'And I think you'll get more. I thought I'd find you somewhere on this highway.'

I slowed down the car. 'How about me? don't I fit the description too?'

The kid almost sneered. 'No. You got brown hair. His is red. Like mine.'

I smiled. 'But I could have dyed it.'

The kid's eyes got wide when he knew what was going to happen.

He was going to be number eight.

All the Needless Killing

by Bryce Walton

He sat eating his regular morning orange and watching the narrow road below through spots of hemlock and pine. Gray and brown stone jutted out in split sections around him, and rose into a jumble of glacial rock blotched with red lichen.

He seemed to doze, but he was alert, listening, hearing everything – particularly the multiple teeming and droning of insect hordes in damp rock and leafy mould, and the flitting of gentle birds in the leaves. There were almost no visitors to this sequestered section at the north end of the lake any more. He would have heard unwanted intruders, but there were none. He heard her station wagon drive in, though, a little after ten, the regular time.

It turned in through the second-growth timber, headed toward the denser wooded area. He stood up, wiped his prim mouth with a clean blue bandanna, brushed dust from his corduroy trousers. Then, holding the handkerchief by opposite corners, he twirled it until it formed a taut effective tool for causing death by strangulation.

There was about him the manner of a mild man. The expression on his thin pale face was bland and his movements usually restrained and paced. But now as he started down through the rocks, he moved with a peculiar surefootedness, in quick, explosive and eager little leaps, suggesting those of a mountain goat.

She got out of the station wagon and stretched, a not unattractive woman whose slight chubbiness made her seem younger than she was, and helped to smooth out what would otherwise have been a few hard lines around her eyes and mouth. She wore slacks, not too tight, hiking boots, a loose khaki blouse with rolled-up sleeves. She had her peroxided hair tied in a pony tail with a red ribbon.

Sunlight through the leaves speckled her with shade. She took a deep breath. It had rained during the night. This morning was cooler than the others had been. Quaint animal life chattered and ran about. Snowdrops were open and forsythia broke in sprays of yellow. All ecstatic stuff for outdoor types, no doubt. But she did not consider herself an outdoor-type girl. Still it was a pleasant moment. And because it was pleasant, it reminded her of the city. She hoped soon to go back to Manhattan. One way or another.

She got the leather bag from the front seat, slid the strap over her shoulder. She opened the back of the station wagon, took out a cigar box lined with cotton, the killing-bottle, and two sandwiches and a thermos of martinis, put them into the bag. Then she got the butterfly net out and swished it delicately in the air.

This might, or might not, be another long unrewarding day. But it would alleviate the nauseating monotony of being the wife of a farmer. Especially a New England farmer, who happened to be wealthy. New England farmers were stereotypes of something; she wasn't quite sure what, except that it was tight-lipped, rigid, narrow and terribly grim. Anything, in a word, but pagan. Still, there were times when a girl, who had not always been blessed with security and leisure, should not complain.

She studied the ripe buzzing air and camp shadows with predatory eyes. A bright yellow butterfly flitted past on a vagrant breath of breeze and she skipped after it, swinging her butterfly net about in what appeared to be that specialized joy reserved only for hunters stalking prey.

At one P.M., she lay down by an aged elm, ate sandwiches, sipped a martini, then stretched out pleasantly tired, and with her forearm over her face, she closed her eyes.

It was the killing-bottle . . .

He watched her through a curtain of briar. His slightly enlarged eyes studied her through thick lenses like those of a microscope. After having watched her loathsome antics for three days, he knew that she possessed exceptional strength and agility for a woman. Overpowering her was out of the question, for he was a rather frail man and detested the physical. If she frightened easily, she would hardly keep coming daily into these so-called ghoul-haunted woods (the local natives were extremely superstitious) to hunt alone, therefore the paralyzed fear reaction could not be depended upon. The surprise attack seemed the only suitable approach.

He watched her until he felt sure she was sleeping soundly. He padded noiselessly in a circle, crept up behind the elm and peered around and down at the reclining figure.

He ran the slightly oily and damp rope of bandanna through his pink hands. He studied the movement, the sound of her breathing. She would hardly be awake before he slipped the handkerchief under her head and brought the ends together and twisted gently. Not too much pressure, of course, slow gentle application reducing consciousness, but not obliterating it. She would lie breathing as though asleep.

He looked at the killing-bottle beside her. It was about the size of an ordinary fruit-jar, perhaps bigger. There was the horrible column of cotton-wool coiling up to the glass stopper. There it was, her lethal chamber, her big-game hunting apparatus.

A slight smile, not so bland upon closer examination, appeared on his lips. There was a hint of cruelty in it. If it was cruelty, it was no ordinary kind, but the reserved, implacable judging and sentencing of a breaker of sacred laws by a creature of righteous wrath.

He slipped on a pair of tight brown suede gloves. She would lie there afterward, still breathing. He would release the stopper and the huntress would snuff up the almond-scented fumes. She wouldn't wake up, wouldn't mind at all because it was a safe and pleasant smell. It was always so difficult to understand why cyanide of potassium should be lethal. But it always was. And one long whiff of it would be all that was required.

He slipped around the tree, over protruding roots. He crouched. The handkerchief stetched taut between his hands. Slip it quickly beneath her head, twist, hold –

The bandanna ducked, slid – scooped empty air!

He fell to his knees off balance, and felt an amazingly light touch along his right arm, a digging under his shoulder. Then the world gyrated. It was a blur. It smeared in a senseless pinwheeling rush of mingled leaves, sky and whirling rocks.

He hit on his upper back with an unpleasant jarring thud. She was leaning against the tree watching him as he sat up and blinked. He felt his neck. He rolled his head around a few times carefully, experimentally. His look, when he saw her, showed fear, but more outraged dignity mixed with sadness. he tensed as though to run away as he stood up.

'I'm sorry,' she said, smiling in a warm but guarded manner. 'But you scared me. I hope you're not hurt.'

'I'm not sure,' he mumbled and spat a fragment of leaf from his lip. He twisted, trying to determine if he was hurt. 'I don't believe so.'

They stared at one another for awhile.

'Sure you're not hurt?' she asked.

He managed a nervous smile and began brushing leaves from shirt and trousers. 'I suppose not.'

Her smile broadened. It was the friendly expression of a thoroughly confident person. 'First time I ever had to really use the old judo. You'd be surprised how many girls are taking it up these days.'

'Yes, it was a surprise.'

'Well, I'm glad there was no harm done.'

His watery distorted eyes blinked at her, then around at brush, trees, and rocks, back to her. He reached down, picked up his horn-rimmed glasses, and put them on. 'Of course I should apologize and I do,' he said, more at ease now. 'Your actions were perfectly understandable. I should explain mine. You see, I was supposed to meet an – ah – friend here. Hardly anyone ever comes in here, so naturally I thought you were she.'

She proffered a pack of cigarettes. He gracefully declined; he didn't use them.

She lit one for herself, and continued to study him with a friendly curiosity. Smoke formed two horns rising from her nostrils.

'Well,' he finally said. 'Again, I'm sorry. But I'd better move along. I don't want to miss my friend.'

'Wait,' she said. 'Would you like a martini?' she lifted the thermos.

He moistened his lips. He shifted uneasily. 'I really shouldn't.'

'Please do; you could use it right now.' She watched his face as she added, 'You see, I know who you intended to meet here. *Me.*'

He tensed again. His eyes widened, bulged slightly. 'What?'

'I wish you wouldn't be afraid,' she said.

'Why – why should I be?'

'That's right, you shouldn't.' She poured a martini into the thermos top and handed it to him.

He took it in a dazed, reflexive gesture and gulped it hastily. His high pale forehead was damp.

'More?'

'I –'

She poured the topful of martini. He sat down heavily on a rock and gripped the drink between both hands.

'I haven't lived in Sawmill County long,' she said in a casual, conversational manner. 'I'm Barbara. What's your name?'

'Jim,' he said in an almost inaudible voice.

'Well, Jim, I came out here to live with my husband right after we were married a few months ago. That's the custom, you know.' She smiled. He flashed a quick dutiful smile in return. Obviously, smiling was hardly one of his regular habits. 'I was curious. I've always been curious. I learned a lot in a short time. One of the first things I heard about was Loon Woods. About how several people died around here during the past two summers.'

Jim sipped his martini and sat rigidly on the edge of the rock.

'Four people. Two last summer, two the summer before. Three women, one man. I love mysteries and I found out more.'

She lit a cigarette.

'Yes,' he said faintly. 'What did you find out?'

'They were of different ages, from various parts of the

county. One, a woman, was from another state. The four who died weren't related. They didn't have a thing in common, Jim, but what they happened to be doing when they died. They were catching butter.lies – with one exception, which isn't really an exception the way I see it. One of them, the man, was catching beetles.'

'If you were that curious, you must have found out more.'

'Oh, yes. But I guessed at things too. The two ladies who died summer before last were found poisoned, poisoned by the fumes from their killing-bottles. The man catching beetles last summer was poisoned by the bite of a water moccasin. The woman that summer was also poisoned by fumes from her killing-bottle. She fell, the bottle broke a few inches from her face; she inhaled the fumes.'

'Something of a coincidence,' Jim said.

'It certainly was, wasn't it? The three women all dying in the same way. Our local Sheriff Reed thought it was simply a coincidence. But then he seems to be a very stupid and complaisant fellow. Not much imagination. The two women summer before last – it was easy to see them as accidents. The two last summer raised doubts in some people's minds, but not Sheriff Reed's.'

'And what about you?' Jim asked. He had finished his second martini. His face was slightly flushed. He started to protest, but mildly, as she poured him a third. 'Thank you, thank you very much,' he said. 'I seem to need these.'

She was watching a number of gaudy butterflies fluttering about in the dappled shade. Her face softened. 'Dear, beautiful, harmless things,' she whispered. 'There's so many of them around here now. People have been scared off from coming in here much, haven't they? Now it's as if those dear gentle things know where they're safe and protected from capture and cruel execution.'

He started. He leaned toward her. His face softened, and his watery eyes seemed brimming with ineffable sadness. 'Yes, they realize they have a refuge here. Many birds do too. This has become a kind of sanctuary.'

She nodded and for awhile they shared an unspoken affinity, with the heat of the day flickering visibly upward from the loam and leaves.

'So,' she said finally. 'What about me, you ask? I'll tell you.

I kept thinking about what those people had in common – their murdering of God's innocent. And because I felt so strongly their evil – I got a hunch, Jim. I got a hunch about how and why they had really died.'

Jim sipped his martini and his face was wistful and at the same time tense with interest. 'Yes, I understand, you know. I, too, see those people as murderers.'

'Of course. A few people realize the sacredness of life, of all life, from the smallest nit to the glorious elephant. Isn't that what you mean?'

His mouth dropped open. He nodded as though partially stunned. 'Oh, yes, yes,' he sighed.

'And I thought about it and there was my hunch. There were facts too, Jim. The poetic justice of their deaths. I knew it wasn't a coincidence. And then I found out that someone had seen a stranger near here twice just after those deaths. A stranger. A stranger because everyone around here knows everyone else. And this stranger couldn't be described exactly. Could have been a number of people. But it wasn't anyone from around here. I decided that those four people had been killed, Jim.'

He couldn't quite pull his fixed gaze from her face. There seemed to be a kind of rapture in her expression as if her own words had placed her under an euphoric spell.

'You see,' she said, with a look of rapture, 'it was more than just a hunch. I understood the need to do what someone had done to those people. I began to feel closer to the – I'd rather not say killer, but executioner. I understood why he did it, the need for justice.'

'You did?' Jim whispered.

'Oh, yes. Before I left the city I belonged to many societies and organizations. We did our best to stop the senseless slaughter of life – especially all the small gentle things that have never harmed anything or anybody. We can do so little, but the few of us who care should do what we can, shouldn't we?'

'Yes.'

'Not just words. Words are no good, are they?'

'No.'

'Blood calls for blood.' She clenched her fists. 'Oh, I hate cruelty more than anything in the world!'

He leaned forward. His eyes were brighter as the cloudiness left them. 'So do I.' Then he shrank back and he kept staring at the killing-bottle and the butterfly net. 'But you've been capturing them too. They suffer so horribly there, shut up in the bottle. I've seen them, how they flutter and beat and break themselves against the glass walls. I've seen them clinging to that ghastly cottonwool. How they strain and gasp for a last breath of living air.'

A look of horror, only hinted at before, now lay full and undisguised upon Jim's face. He slid away from her across the rock, still clutching the top of the thermos.

She shook her head slowly. Her smile was sad and compassionate. 'You don't understand, Jim. I wanted to meet someone else who felt as I did. I wanted to meet you. That's why I've come out here almost every day for the last month. I guessed that you might come here once in awhile to guard your sanctuary. Now I've found you, and you've found me.'

'You lie,' he said softly. 'You're lying. This is some kind of a trap, isn't it?'

'Please!' She seemed almost on the verge of crying. 'You must believe the truth, Jim. I've often felt like doing what was done to those vile, vicious people. But I never had the courage. Someone did, somewhere, I knew. I wanted to know that person.'

'No, no!' He sat rigidly balanced on the edge of the rock. He started to sip more of the martini, but stopped – as though it had suddenly became distasteful. 'You're like the others. You didn't mind murdering those lovely things, just to find me, and trap me.'

'There's no one else around. No one has ever followed me, Jim, you know that.'

He didn't answer.

'And even if I was an expert at judo, would I come out here alone to trap someone most people would regard as a vicious murderer?'

'Vicious – that isn't true. They died painlessly. That's more than can be said for the countless helpless creatures they tortured and killed!'

'I know that, Jim. Believe me. I know you could never be cruel. I know that you're dedicated to fighting cruelty, and avenging the gentle small things of this world. I am too, Jim. Believe me, I am too. Please believe me. Look.'

She opened the cigar box. She walked toward him slowly, and he sat trembling with some odd hypersensitivity. He glanced reluctantly into the box.

'I've only caught a few, Jim. And they're all cabbage butterflies, don't you see?'

He nodded slowly.

'There are some kinds of butterflies that are dangerous pests, Jim. You must admit it. Just as there are locusts that destroy. There are mosquitoes and other kinds of pests. Only man kills for pleasure, but there are harmful kinds among all species. Isn't that true?'

He hesitated, then gave a quick nod of assent. But he wouldn't look at the box any more. 'Undeniably, you're right,' he said. 'Yes, you're right about the cabbage butterfly. And there are other noxious insects that should be destroyed, just as is the case with men.'

'But there are not many insects that deserve such a fate, Jim. And you can see that I've caught only the harmful ones.'

'Yes. The list of destructive lepidoptera is relatively insignificant.' He seemed to relax a little. She refreshed his martini, and he began to sip again.

His face was soon flushed, and his breathing fast. She put her hand over his hand, and they sat there together side by side on the rock holding hands for some time, communing in an inner quiet that seemed flawless and unbreakable.

Then they finished the batch of martinis and talked in excited discovery of one another. He talked about the brief but glorious life of the butterflies and other insects, how they lived their own brilliant but strange cycle in only a few hours sometimes, to finally be killed by nature's way, by the frost. Everything had been planned to balance out, and man was destroying the balance, destroying the world itself.

She asked him again to trust her. She would be back again tomorrow, she said. He could meet her there in the same place. He could watch, be certain she was not followed, finally be convinced that she was not part of any sort of trap.

They met there the next day. She waited over an hour under the elm until suddenly he appeared, moving out of the leaves silently. She had two thermos bottles of martinis this time, and they enjoyed themselves with a steady lessening of strain and suspicion.

He talked about when summer would be over; the blossoms would come to seed and the fledglings to flight. The knowing squirrel was already hoarding its winter harvest. Soon feathered migrants would be heading south and the cricket would seek a sheltered place. The sun would cross the celestial equator, he said, and summer would be officially dismissed. But the squirrels, chipmunks and woodchucks and robins knew nothing of these precise hours or minutes. They did well enough, he said, without clocks or calendars. He felt it in his blood too, he said, just as they did. And just as she did, she was quick to point out. No need to check anything by manmade instruments of measurement to know. Indeed not, she said. They didn't have to look at the sun's shadow. How unimportant precise moments were, he said, except in man's statistics.

Cause and effect, nature's cosmic balance. Man was destroying it all.

'God, Jim,' she said with an almost savage intensity, 'if we could only do more to save millions of little lives.'

They met the next day, the day after, and then almost every day. Soon he was waiting for her. It was a lonely world for their kind, they agreed. They sat until the sun went down and the cicada droning of the hot afternoon began to fade and the insect chorus began.

She pointed out a dead robin, then another.

'You know what killed them?' she said. 'What is killing birds by the thousands every day, Jim?'

He caressed the small inert puff of feathers, then turned away.

'Man is killing them, Jim. The farmers around here are killing everything with their pumps of poison sprays. You know that, don't you?'

'Oh, yes, I know that!'

'Every day, Jim, with their pumps and vile hoses smearing poison over the land. Millions – billions even – are being killed now. It poisons the larvae and pupae and they never are allowed to live. And that kills the birds too, because they eat the insects and the larvae. That's what kills these robins, you know.'

'I know.' He sank down to his knees and remained there for some time, his head bowed.

She whispered with a harshly accusing tone. 'We're quibblers and piddlers, Jim. We are, you know. You made your gesture, didn't you, but how insignificant it was compared with what they do every day. They slaughter millions every day. And you've struck back, yes, but what have you and I accomplished? Four people! They didn't use sprays. They killed a few, but how does that compare with the billions that are being slaughtered here day in and day out?'

'I know, I know,' he moaned softly. He raised small clenched fists. 'What can I do? I used to try to convince others. I published pamphlets. I made speeches at the university, but they laughed at me finally. People think I'm abnormal in some way, a kind of – well – a crackpot. That's what they say about our kind. I can only do a little. Sometimes it seems to be driving me crazy because I'm alone and helpless and frustrated and no one cares!'

'Now you listen,' she said and turned him around and they looked steadily into each other's face. 'You can do a great deal more. With one act you can save millions and millions of sacred little lives.'

As she continued talking and he listened, his eyes grew abnormally bright behind his thick-lensed glasses. He bent slightly forward and his breath came faster. He kept nodding in agreement, his head moving in quick jerking little motions like a bird's.

'I know their habits,' she said. 'I can help. I know when they work and where to find them. I'll tell you when and where to strike!'

'Not a few,' he whispered. 'But millions and billions saved. The birds saved!'

'Yes, yes!'

He began to sway in a subtle rhythm to the intensity of his feelings as she gave him vital information. The insect chorus rose around him. It was only a whispering of the wind and the rustling of leaves at first. Then it swelled from the throats of the most abundant life on earth, the pygmy hordes celebrating their season in the sun, the late afternoon of their life.

The insect chorus rose in his ears like thunder, the humming, scratching, singing drone swelled and seemed to explode in his head ...

He was there in the storage shed, under the damp corrugated tin roof, early. He was there alert and ready before five A.M. Above him on a rack of two-by-four planks were the barrels of deadly parathion used to spray crops, used to heartlessly slaughter millions of sacred living things. A few pests must be killed, therefore go on and kill everything, kill all the beautiful gentle things, kill the butterflies and velvet-winged moths, kill the beautiful Swallowtail and the Macaons and Purple Emperors and lovely iridescent peacock-winged Pavitos, kill the Holly Blues, and the Tornoasoladas and magnificent golden-wing Tortoiseshells. And finally there would be nothing, nothing but silence where the robins had once come back in the spring.

He stood in the shadows waiting, with the spray tank beside him and the nozzle ready in his hand. A tinge of dawn filtered through the cracks in the shed and he heard the plaintive screech of a barn owl and then the back screen door of the farmhouse snapped shut.

He waited and listened to the clopping of heavy shoes approaching the door of the shed.

It did not matter who it was, of course. He was one of the killers and soon he would die so that millions might live. Blood calls for blood. The workings of justice are indeed secret and incalculable. This one now, and the others later, one by one. He remembered what she had told him and she was so right about it, about so many things. There was enough poison in one small killing-bottle to kill the inhabitants of an entire town. But how to administer it? How much more logical it was to select those who were directly responsible for the indiscriminate murder of millions, eliminate them on the spot. Painlessly of course, or comparatively painlessly, and with poetic justice, as she had pointed out, with their own vile, suffocating, poisonous spray!

He peered through a crack between the warped boards. He saw a shadowy figure only a few yards from the shed now, a tall man in a straw hat with a ragged brim, a pair of levis, a faded blue denim jacket.

Jim inhaled deeply and raised the handle of the spray pump. That man was not at all a hated object. He could be regarded objectively, without malice, merely as a thing to be eliminated for purposes that no sane man should reasonably question.

The man stepped through the doorway. He stopped, startled, uncertain. Jim pushed down the pump handle and a pale stream caught the man flush and hissing in the face. The man screamed and clawed at his eyes. He ran blindly into the side of the shed and fell as Jim coolly continued to pump while aiming the nozzle with unerring accuracy and singleness of purpose.

Barbara sat pale and tearless at the kitchen table, as if too shocked, too stunned, to cry. Sheriff Reed watched her with awkward sympathy, his small black eyes in a procine face avoiding her direct gaze. He finished the coffee in one sucking gulp and stood up.

'Better get that fella into the town jail,' he said. 'Guess I better.'

'More coffee?' she asked listlessly.

'No, thank you, Ma'am. I got here quick as I could when you telephoned. But I guess I couldn't have helped much nohow.'

'No one could have done anything,' she said. 'A few drops of parathion on the skin can kill a person in minutes if they don't get treatment. My – my husband was just drowned in it by that – that awful person!'

'Well, we got him, Ma'am, thanks to you. Pretty good shootin', only it's kind of a good thing you didn't hit him in a vital spot. That would have been too easy on him.'

'Darrell thought it was a robber and went out to see,' she said. 'That was all –'

'I reckon he was at least a thief. He don't look like no thief though. Identification says he's a college professor from over in Lakeville.'

'He – he must have been crazy or something,' she said thinly.

'Can't ever tell about people.'

'I don't care. I've lost my Darrell!' She turned away and bit her lip.

'Fine man,' Sheriff Reed said. 'Hard worker and steady as a rock. Never harmed nobody. Well –' he hesitated. '– he was a good provider and I reckon he left you comfortable set up – I mean moneywise?'

She nodded. The farm plus fifty thousand in insurance was indeed comforting. She would sell the farm, rent a penthouse on Park Avenue. No more scrounging for television roles or being a stand-in for much less talented actresses than herself. If she still felt so inclined, she would buy a lead in a Broadway show, and –

She put her head down on her folded arms and began to cry.

Sheriff Reed patted her shoulder. 'You just let it all out now, Ma'am, that's what you need. I'll take that fellow on in. Why, the poor guy's liable to bleed plumb to death. And you're right, I think he's buggy. He won't say anything. Every time you pick him up he falls down on his hands and knees again.'

She seemed too broken up to answer. He backed quietly out the kitchen door.

There was some claim to his being insane.

But he was articulate and disclaimed any inability to distinguish right from wrong.

He knew very well right from wrong and passionately explained how right he had been in killing people ...

They strapped down his wrists to the arms of the chair. His ankles were clamped. Steel doors slammed. He stared at the glass enclosure of the chamber. Faces studied him curiously through the glass, and the faces began to blur as if the glass were steaming over.

He hadn't realized for some time what was really happening to him. It was as though he had been sleep-walking and had suddenly awakened.

And now he knew.

He knew when the cyanide pellets dropped into a bucket of acid under his chair and the fumes drifted up into a mist before his face.

He smelled the fumes and he saw the faces pressing against the glass and watching him through the glass and he knew well enough.

It was the killing-bottle.

The Explosives Expert

by John Lutz

Billy Edgemore, the afternoon bartender, stood behind the long bar of the Last Stop Lounge and squinted through the dimness at the sunlight beyond the front window. He was a wiry man, taller than he appeared at first, and he looked like he should be a bartender, with his bald head, cheerfully seamed face and his brilliant red vest that was the bartender's uniform at the Last Stop. Behind him long rows of glistening bottles picked up the light on the mirrored backbar, the glinting clear gins and vodkas, the beautiful amber bourbons and lighter Scotches, the various hues of the assorted wines, brandies and liqueurs. The Last Stop's bar was well stocked.

Beyond the ferns that blocked the view out (and in) the front window, Billy saw a figure cross the small patch of light and turn to enter the stained-glass front door, the first customer he was to serve that day.

It was Sam Daniels. Sam was an employee of the Hulton Plant up the street, as were most of the customers of the Last Stop.

'Afternoon, Sam,' Billy said, turning on his professional smile. 'Kind of early today, aren't you?'

'Off work,' Sam said, mounting a bar stool as if it were a horse. 'Beer.'

Billy drew a beer and set the wet schooner in front of Sam on the mahogany bar. 'Didn't expect a customer for another two hours, when the plant lets out,' Billy said.

'Guess not,' Sam said, sipping his beer. He was a short man with a swarthy face, a head of curly hair, and a stomach paunch too big for a man in his early thirties – a man who liked his drinking.

'Figured you didn't go to work when I saw you weren't wearing your badge,' Billy said. The Hulton Plant manufactured some secret government thing, a component for the hydrogen bomb, and each employee had to wear his small plastic badge with his name, number and photograph on it in order to enter or leave the plant.

'Regular Sherlock,' Sam said, and jiggled the beer in his glass.

'You notice lots of things when you're a bartender,' Billy said, wiping down the bar with a clean white towel. You notice things, Billy repeated to himself, and you get to know people, and when you get to know them, really get to know them, you've got to dislike them. 'I guess I tended bar in the wrong places.'

'What's that?' Sam Daniels asked.

'Just thinking out loud,' Billy said, and hung the towel on its chrome rack. When Billy looked at his past he seemed to be peering down a long tunnel of empty bottles, drunks and hollow laughter; of curt orders, see-through stares and dreary conversations. He'd never liked his job, but it was all he'd known for the past thirty years.

'Wife's supposed to meet me here pretty soon,' Sam said. 'She's getting off work early.' He winked at Billy. 'Toothache.'

Billy smiled his automatic smile and nodded. He never had liked Sam, who had a tendency to get loud and violent when he got drunk.

Within a few minutes Rita Daniels entered. She was a tall, pretty woman, somewhat younger than her husband. She had a good figure, dark eyes, and expensively bleached blonde hair that looked a bit stringy now from the heat outside.

'Coke and bourbon,' she ordered, without looking at Billy. He served her the highball where she sat next to her husband at the bar.

No one spoke for a while as Rita sipped her drink. The faint sound of traffic, muffled through the thick door of the Last Stop, filled the silence. When a muted horn sounded, Rita said, 'It's dead in here. Put a quarter in the jukebox.'

Sam did as his wife said, and soft jazz immediately displaced the traffic sounds.

'You know I don't like jazz, Sam.' Rita downed her drink quicker than she should have, then got down off the stool to go the powder room.

'Saw Doug Baker last night,' Billy said, picking up the empty glass. Doug Baker was a restaurant owner who lived on the other side of town, and it was no secret that he came to the Last Stop only to see Rita Daniels, though Rita was almost always with her husband.

'How 'bout that,' Sam said. 'Two more of the same.'

Rita returned to her stool, and Billy put two highballs before her and her husband.

'I was drinking beer,' Sam said in a loud voice.

'So you were,' Billy answered, smiling his My Mistake smile. He shrugged and motioned toward the highballs. 'On the house. Unless you'd rather have beer.'

'No,' Sam said, 'think nothing of it.'

That was how Billy thought Sam would answer. His cheapness was one of the things Billy disliked most about the man. It was one of the things he knew Rita disliked most in Sam Daniels too.

'How'd it go with the hydrogen bombs today?' Rita asked her husband. 'Didn't go in at all, huh?'

Billy could see she was aggravated and was trying to nag him.

'No,' Sam said, 'and I don't make hydrogen bombs.'

'Ha!' Rita laughed. 'You oughta think about it. That's about all you can make.' She turned away before Sam could answer. 'Hey, Billy, you know anything about hydrogen bombs?'

'Naw,' Billy said. 'Your husband knows more about that than me.'

'Yeah,' Rita said, 'the union rates him an expert. Some expert! Splices a few wires together.'

'Five dollars an hour,' Sam said, 'and double time for overtime.'

Rita whirled a braceleted arm above her head. 'Wheee...'

Like many married couples, Sam and Rita never failed to bicker when they came into the Last Stop. Billy laughed. 'The Friendly Daniels.' Sam didn't laugh.

'Don't bug me today,' Sam said to Rita. 'I'm in a bad mood.'

'Cheer up, Sam,' Billy said. 'It's a sign she loves you, or loves somebody, anyway.'

Sam ignored Billy and finished his drink. 'Where'd you go last night?' he asked his wife.

'You know I was at my sister's. I even stopped in here for about a half hour on the way. Billy can verify it.'

'Right,' Billy said.

'I thought you said Doug Baker was in here last night,' Sam said to him, his eyes narrow.

'He was,' Billy said. 'He, uh, came in late.' He turned to make more drinks, placing the glasses lip to lip and pouring bourbon into each in one deft stream without spilling a drop. He made them a little stronger this time, shooting in the soda expertly, jabbing swizzle sticks between the ice cubes and placing the glasses on the bar.

'You wouldn't be covering up or anything, would you, Billy?' Sam's voice had acquired a mean edge.

'Now *wait a minute!*' Rita said. 'If you think I came in here last night to see Doug Baker, you're crazy!'

'Well,' Sam stirred his drink viciously and took a sip, 'Billy mentioned Baker was in here ...'

'I said he came in late,' Billy said quickly.

'And he acted like he was covering up or something,' Sam said, looking accusingly at Billy.

'*Covering up?*' Rita turned to Billy, her penciled eyebrows knitted in a frown. 'Have you ever seen me with another man?'

'Naw,' Billy said blandly, 'of course not. You folks shouldn't fight.'

Still indignant, Rita swiveled on her stool to face her husband. 'Have I ever been unfaithful?'

'How the hell should I know?'

'Good point,' Billy said with a forced laugh.

'It's not funny!' Rita snapped.

'Keep it light, folks,' Billy said seriously. 'You know we don't like trouble in here.'

'Sorry,' Rita said, but her voice was hurt. She swiveled back to face the bar and gulped angrily on her drink. Billy could see that the liquor was getting to her, was getting to them both.

There was silence for a while, then Rita said morosely 'I *oughta* go out on you, Mr. Five-dollar-hydrogen-bomb-expert! You think I do anyway, and at least Doug Baker's got money.'

Sam grabbed her wrist, making the bracelets jingle. She tried to jerk away but he held her arm so tightly that his knuckles were white. 'You ever see Baker behind my back and I'll kill you both!' He almost spit the words out.

'Hey, now,' Billy said gently, 'don't talk like that, folks!' He placed his hand on Sam Daniels' arm and felt the muscles relax as Sam released his wife. She bent over silently on her stool and held the wrist as if it were broken. 'Have one on the house,' Billy said, taking up their almost empty glasses. 'One to make up by.'

'Make mine straight,' Sam said. He was breathing hard and his face was red.

'*Damn you!*' Rita moaned. She half fell off the stool and walked quickly but staggeringly to the powder room again.

Billy began to mix the drinks deftly, speedily, as if there were a dozen people at the bar and they all demanded service. In the faint red glow from the beer-ad electric clock he looked like an ancient alchemist before his rows of multicolored bottles. 'You shouldn't be so hard on her,' he said absently as he mixed. 'Can't believe all the rumours you hear about a woman as pretty as Rita, and a harmless kiss in fun never hurt nobody.'

'Rumors?' Sam leaned over the bar. 'Kiss? What kiss? Did she kiss Baker last night?'

'Take it easy,' Billy said. 'I told you Baker came in late.' The phone rang, as it always did during the fifteen minutes before the Hulton Plant let out, with wives leaving messages and asking for errant husbands. When Billy returned, Rita was back at the bar.

'Let's get out of here,' she said. There were tear streaks in her makeup.

'Finish your drinks and go home happy, folks.' Billy shot a glance at the door and set the glasses on the bar.

Rita drank hers slowly, but Sam tossed his drink down

and stared straight ahead. Quietly, Billy put another full glass in front of him.

'I hear you *were* in here with Baker last night,' Sam said in a low voice. 'Somebody even saw you kissing him.'

'You're *crazy!*' Rita's thickened voice was outraged.

Billy moved quickly toward them. 'I didn't say that.'

'I knew you were covering up!' Sam glared pure hate at him. 'We'll see what Baker says, because I'm going to drive over to his place right now and bash his brains out!'

'*But I didn't even see Baker last night!*' Rita took a pull on her drink, trying to calm herself. Sam swung sharply around with his forearm, hitting Rita's chin and the highball glass at the same time. There was a clink as the glass hit her teeth and she fell backward off the stool.

Billy reached under the bar and his hand came up with a glinting chrome automatic that seemed to catch every ray of light in the place. It was a gentleman's gun, and standing there in his white shirt and red vest Billy looked like a gentleman holding it.

'Now, don't move, folks.' He aimed the gun directly at Sam's stomach. 'You know we don't go for that kind of trouble in here.' He looked down and saw blood seeping between Rita's fingers as she held her hand over her mouth. Billy wet a clean towel and tossed it to her, and she held it to her face and scooted backward to sit sobbing in the farthest booth.

Billy leaned close to Sam. 'Listen,' he said, his voice a sincere whisper, 'I don't want to bring trouble on Baker, or on you for that matter, so I can't stand by and let you go over there and kill him and throw your own life away. It wasn't him she was in here with. He came in later.'

'Wasn't him?' Sam asked in bewildered fury. 'Who was it then?'

'I don't know,' Billy said, still in a whisper so Rita couldn't hear. 'He had a badge on, so he worked at the plant, but I don't know who he is and that's the truth.'

'*Oh, no!*'

'Take it easy, Sam. She only kissed him in that booth there. And I'm not even sure I saw that. The booth was dark.'

Sam tossed down the drink that was on the bar and

moaned. He was staring at the automatic and Billy could see he wanted desperately to move.

A warm silence filled the bar, and then the phone rang shrilly, turning the silence to icicles.

'Now take it easy,' Billy said, backing slowly down the bar toward the phone hung on the wall. 'A kiss isn't anything.' As the phone rang again he could almost see the shrill sound grate through Sam's tense body. Billy placed the automatic on the bar and took the last five steps to the phone. He let it ring once more before answering it.

'Naw,' Billy said into the receiver, standing with his back to Sam and Rita, 'he's not here.' He stood for a long moment instead of hanging up, as if someone were still on the other end of the line.

The shot was a sudden, angry bark.

Billy put the receiver on the hook and turned. Sam was standing slumped with a supporting hand on a bar stool. Rita was crumpled on the floor beneath the table of the booth she'd been sitting in, her eyes open, her blonde hair bright with blood.

His head still bowed, Sam began to shake.

Within minutes the police were there, led by a young plainclothes detective named Parks.

'You say they were arguing and he just up and shot her?' Parks was asking as his men led Sam outside.

'He accused her of running around,' Billy said. 'They were arguing, he hit her, and I was going to throw them out when the phone rang. I set the gun down for a moment when I went to answer the phone, and he grabbed it and shot.'

'Uh-hm,' Parks said efficiently, flahing a look toward where Rita's body had lain before they'd photographed it and taken it away. 'Pretty simple, I guess. Daniels confessed as soon as we got here. In fact, we couldn't shut him up. Pretty broken.'

'Who wouldn't be?' Billy said.

'Save some sympathy for the girl.' Parks looked around. 'Seems like a nice place. I don't know why there's so much trouble in here.'

Billy shrugged. 'In a dive, a class joint or a place like this, people are mostly the same.'

Parks grinned. 'You're probably right,' he said, and started toward the door. Before pushing it open, he paused and turned. 'If you see anything like this developing again, give us a call, huh?'

'Sure,' Billy said, polishing a glass and holding it up to the fading afternoon light. 'You know we don't like trouble in here.'

The 79 Murders of Martha Hill Gibbs

by Joseph Csida

In the thirty-nine years I served on the Police Force, from foot patrolman through Commissioner, until I retired in 1955 at the age of sixty-five, I would estimate that I was directly or indirectly involved with slightly over 4000 matricides, uxoricides, filicides, fratricides, parricides and homicides of every conceivable description. Right after I was promoted to Detective Second Grade, while still quite a young man, I was personally responsible for solving a very complex case in which a psychotic chemist killed his wife by injecting bubonic plague germs into her vein, and I have sat in a hundred times on the breaking of the more common dull-witted felon who beats his innocent and generally weaker victim to death with his fists or whatever other blunt instrument he finds at hand.

In all those years, apart from official reports, I have never written a single word about any of these homicides. Now at seventy-one when writing comes quite hard to me, both because it is difficult for me to concentrate as I did when my brain was more nimble, and because the arthritic condition afflicting my hands makes it painful to hold this pencil tightly for more than a half hour or so at a time . . . now I find I *must* write the complete story of these recent deaths.

You note I do not call them homicides. I do not because I do not know whether or not they were homicides.

And if they were homicides I do not know whether the homicides were perpetrated by human hand or by some supernatural force.

It is to attempt to clarify these haunting questions in my

own mind that I write this story at all. I have not slept a full night for three weeks, and I am not sure I will again until I feel I have exhausted every effort to determine what crimes were committed and by whom.

Until Martha Hill Gibbs herself died last week, I could not have brought myself to write this essay at all. Martha Hill Gibbs was one of my oldest and dearest friends, and as fine a woman as I have ever known. If you read detective and mystery stories at all you yourself must surely feel as though you, too, know Martha Hill Gibbs.

She was often called the American Agatha Christie. She wrote her first detective novel, featuring Nurse Mary Brown, in 1921. That year she just wrote the one novel, since she was doing a full-time job as a reporter on *The News* to pay her husband's way through medical school. But every year from that point on, right up until this year, she wrote two complete detective novels each and every year, not to mention countless short stories. You were probably a Nurse Brown fan, just as many people today are Perry Mason fans. Or more likely you are a Chuck Silk, Hollywood actor-private detective fan, since Martha stopped writing the Nurse Brown stories about 1946, and has concentrated almost entirely on Chuck Silk since then.

(But I ramble. You must forgive this terrible weakness of an old man, this tendency to ramble. I will try not to do it.)

As I said, I could never have brought myself to write this story while Martha was alive, no matter what the urgency. And now that I have embarked on the task, I find I hardly know where to begin. Perhaps that morning about six months ago, when Martha phoned to tell me that her husband, and my life-long good friend, Dr. Edward Gibbs had died, is the best place to begin. As I think back on it, it does seem to me that it was shortly after Ed's death that Martha began to act peculiarly.

It was 6:02 that morning when my phone rang. I put down my toothbrush, rinsed my mouth, went into the bedroom and picked up the phone.

'Frank?' Martha said, 'Frank, Ed's dead. Please come over.' There was no hysteria in her deep, resonant voice, just sadness and weariness.

I live diagonally across The Hemlocks from the Gibbs', so it didn't take me more than five minutes to get over. The front door was open, and I walked in, and went up to the bedroom.

Martha was sitting on the side of the bed, holding Ed's hand. Ed was lying on his back, a soft, pleasant smile on his lips, his eyes closed as though in most relaxed sleep.

'You haven't really gone away, Eddie, have you?' she was murmuring. 'I don't want you to go away.'

Then she saw me.

'Ed's dead,' she said again, quietly, rising from the bed. Martha was a tall woman, about 5' 10". She was never really beautiful, but rather handsome and efficient. Ed's death seemed to have caused her to shrink in a strange way. 'But he hasn't really gone away, has he, Frank?' she said now.

I consoled her as best I could. We called our mutual friend, Dr. Goldstein. Ed had died quietly in his sleep of a heart failure. Since he was seventy-five years old, and both he and Martha had had a coronary condition for a number of years, his death came as no real surprise to any of us. But surprise or no surprise, there is always a measure of shock, no matter what the deceased's age, and when people love each other as deeply and genuinely for almost forty years as did Ed and Martha Gibbs, there is also a fierce if quiet heartbreak.

Miss Schmidt, Martha's secretary, and I made all the arrangements for the services and the funeral. I myself broke the news to the Gibbs' granddaughter, Sue, who was away in her first year of college in Los Angeles. Sue is practically like my own granddaughter, just as my own son and daughter, now doing well in Tokyo and Ypsilanti, Michigan, respectively, grew up viewing Ed and Martha Hill Gibbs as a second father and mother.

It was right after the funeral that Martha again displayed the odd new attitude she was developing. Sue, who is seventeen, and Martha and I were in the kitchen of the Gibbs' house, quietly sitting at the table with coffee Sue had just made. Sue was still crying, dry and invisible but very real inner tears.

'Now,' she said, 'now ... Gramp won't be able to come to my wedding.'

'Of course he will, sweetheart,' Martha said in her husky, almost baritone voice.

'What wedding?' I asked. 'I didn't know you were going to get married, Sue ... Martha, you never mentioned it.'

Martha looked at me in a most startled manner for a moment. Then she looked at Sue.

'Yes, Susie dear,' she said. 'What wedding? You never mentioned a wedding to me ... And of course Gramp will be there.'

Sue reached across the table and took Martha's hand.

'I'm sorry, Gram,' she said, and looking at me, 'I'm sorry, Uncle Frank, it's terribly selfish of me. But Charlie Silk and I are planning to get married next month.'

Martha again looked startled.

'Charlie Silk?' she said. 'You can't mean Charlie Silk. He's my detective, and of course Gramp will be there.'

That sounds even more peculiar than it is, or than I mean it to sound. Charlie Silk, as I mentioned earlier and as you know, is the detective character Martha created, just as Erle Stanley Gardner created Perry Mason, or Agatha Christie created Hercule Poirot or Arthur Conan Doyle created Sherlock Holmes.

As a matter of fact, the Charlie Silk TV series is doing almost as well as the Perry Mason series, they tell me. But there is also a real Charlie Silk. Somebody discovered him last fall when Martha and Ed went out to Hollywood to get the Charlie TV film series launched. This Charlie Silk was a private investigator who doubled as a bit-part actor and vice versa.

For a time it looked like he would actually play the Charlie Silk part in the series. But Martha told me later that he was too incompetent an actor, and she didn't like him generally.

The series' producer, however, did use the real Charlie Silk quite extensively in publicity in connection with the series at the time. And I think it was then that Silk met Sue Gibbs, since she had gone out with her grandparents to enroll in school out there.

This particular evening, following the funeral, Martha made some vague, sometimes gentle, sometimes aggressive objections to Sue's marrying Silk, but finally she dropped the subject. She also mentioned repeatedly that Gramp would not like the idea at all, but she finally told Sue not to worry, that Gramp would come to the wedding anyway. I was rather upset to see Martha so distraught and so obviously thrown off her balance by Ed's death. Over the next several weeks, even after Sue went back to school, the situation did not improve. If anything it became worse.

I visited Martha each day, and on each visit she would go on at great length about her conversations with Ed and their plans for the future. Once I walked into the house, and as I approached her study through the living room, I heard her saying:

'Mr. Grau, you are being utterly ridiculous. There is a very substantial difference between murdering someone for profit, and a State execution of that murderer. Murder is not merely murder no matter what the circumstances. I do not necessarily believe there is any such thing as justifiable homicide ...'

I walked into the study. Martha was sitting at her desk. She was speaking to the empty chair at the side of the desk.

I said, 'Hello, Martha,' and she turned slowly and smiled.

'Frank,' she said, 'how nice you could come. I was just talking with Mr. Grau.'

I tried to hide my bafflement, but apparently didn't succeed, for she said:

'You know Mr. Grau, of course. He was the murderer in *Death on the Dixie Highway*. He killed that lovely young couple from Alabama.'

You may remember *Death on the Dixie Highway*. I think it was one of the best Martha had ever done. Mr. Grau was a particularly cunning killer. As I remembered him, a kindly gentleman of about sixty with a surprisingly luxuriant head of white hair and handlebar mustache to match. But Mr. Grau was a character in a seven-year-old novel, not a real person sitting in Martha's study. At least I thought so then.

I joined the conversation with the invisible Mr. Grau and Martha long enough to humor her out of it, then discussed a new rose bush I had planted that morning. I also spent about an hour and a half trying to persuade Martha to begin a new book. I felt that if I could get her immersed in her writing again, an occupation which she truly loved, it would help her. At one point in this discussion she smiled sweetly at me and said:

'I have the most wonderful plot, Frank, but I don't believe I'll write this one.'

And the next morning – it was a Sunday – Martha disappeared.

About seven-thirty that morning, I was out trimming the rose bush I had discussed with her when a very well kept and polished ebony limousine pulled up across the street directly in front of the Gibbs' house. I put down my shears and put on my glasses. The car looked like a 1927 model of the kind the more affluent gangsters of that era sported. And as I looked a thin, tall, swarthy man stepped out of the car on the driver's side and came around to the opposite side, the side facing the Gibbs' house. He was, ridiculously enough, dressed in a loud, light-colored suit and white panama hat. He, like the automobile, looked like a tin horn but successful gangster or gambler of the late twenties.

I peered at him, and had the strange feeling that I knew him. Just then Martha came out of the door. She waved to me as she strode down the path. She seemed to walk more briskly and with more vitality than at any time since Ed's death.

'Good morning, Frank,' she sang. I use that word advisedly, because that is virtually what she did, and this was the first time Martha had sounded of good cheer since Ed's passing. The tall man held the door open for her, she stepped into the car, he went around to the driver's side and they drove off. Martha waved again as they pulled away. I don't know why, but I noted the license number.

About four that afternoon Miss Schmidt called me.

'Mr. Malloy,' she said, 'did Mrs. Gibbs tell you she was going to be away today?'

'No,' I said. 'Why?'

'Well, she asked me to come in at my regular time today, about ten o'clock, and when I got here she was gone. I've been through the mail, and in addition to the normal correspondence and bills and solicitations, I found something very peculiar.'

'What?'

'There's a note here ... It says: "We are having a very special reunion and would be greatly honored if you would join us. Johnny French will pick you up at 7.30 A.M., Sunday, August 11, if you care to attend our meeting."

'And it's signed,' said Miss Schmidt, '"Affectionately, Your Murderers."'

A number of thoughts ran through my mind. I thought: Very interesting, she's plotting a new story. I thought: Johnny French, Johnny French, that's a very familiar name. I thought about the tall, thin swarthy man from 1927.

As I have said, Martha Hill Gibbs and Ed, and my deceased wife, Ann, and I were close friends ever since we were all in our twenties. I got to know Martha originally when she came to see me at police headquarters to ask whether I would help her with some technical information she needed for her first detective novel.

Miss Schmidt said, rather anxiously, 'Mr. Malloy, Mr. Malloy, are you there ... Mr. Malloy!'

I didn't realize that I hadn't said anything for a long, long moment. And then it flashed through my mind that Johnny French was the murderer in the very first detective novel Martha Hill Gibbs wrote. And that the description of Johnny French, as I remembered it, fitted perfectly the description of the tall, thin swarthy man who had come to call for Martha that morning.

'Don't get excited, Miss Schmidt,' I said, 'and leave everything just the way it is. I'll be right over.'

The arthritic pain in my hand and wrist and lower right arm is so intense now that I shall have to stop writing for a moment, but it is just as well. I need a little time to think again. About the fact that first I had come upon Martha having a conversation with Mr. Grau, one of her murderers, invisible though he was. And now I had *seen* Martha drive off with another of her murderers, Johnny French. A quite visible and real person. Quite possibly, I am forced to admit, Johnny French!

When I hung up the phone after talking to Miss Schmidt I took a moment to look up *The Wheel Stops at Murder,* Martha's first detective novel, in my library. I was right. The murderer's name was Johnny French and he looked precisely like the man who had picked Martha up that morning. And in the novel he drove a very expensive ebony limousine.

'I'm so glad you're here,' Miss Schmidt said, as I walked into the study. 'Here's the note.'

She handed me a rolled document. Unrolled it measured approximately four by six inches. It was like no paper I had ever seen or felt. It was like no parchment either. And yet it was not exactly cloth. At the risk of seeming hysterical, I can only describe its color as an eerie blue. I did not know then, and have never found out, just what kind of material it was. The message Miss Schmidt had read me was typed neatly in the center of the material. I say typed, although I do not know that for sure either. The letters looked as though they had been typewritten rather than printed or handwritten. They were of a strangely faint gray or silver color.

In carefully interrogating Miss Schmidt I ascertained that as far as Miss Schmidt had been able to discover the document had simply appeared on Martha's desk. That is to say that while all the other mail of the day had been in envelopes, stamped and postmarked, this document had merely been lying in the center of the desk. A very thorough search by Miss Schmidt through the waste baskets also revealed no container in which the rolled message might have come.

I told Miss Schmidt she could go home. I made up my mind that if Martha was not back by the following morning I would call in the police. She did not return by the following morning, and so, at my request, a young officer of about fifty, a Sergeant from the Missing Persons Bureau, met me at the Gibbs House.

Naturally I did not tell him anything about Martha's behavior. I merely told him in the most explicit detail about her departure, described the man who had picked her up, and gave him the license number and rolled message which Miss Schmidt had found on her desk. I asked the young man, Sergeant Otto Hunseker, to keep me informed as to whatever progress he made, and he promised he would. He was as good as his word. It wasn't a full twenty-four hours later that he called me.

'Commissioner,' he said. 'This is Sergeant Hunseker. We found the limousine in a parking lot out at Idlewild. The owner is a Herman Grau and we're looking for him now. And we've found witnesses who saw the tall thin man you described escort Mrs. Gibbs to the gate for a jet flight to Los Angeles. So far we haven't found the man himself, nor anyone who saw Mrs. Gibbs after she got off the plane in L.A. I'm sure she's all right, though, and as soon as we find out anything more I'll let you know.'

I thanked the Sergeant. But I was still quite worried. At the time it seemed to me utterly ridiculous that a name, Herman Grau, the same as the murderer in Martha's story, should pop up again. I called Sue Gibbs in Los Angeles, on the pretext of wishing to know how she was coming along in her studies, and how her wedding plans were progressing. Since I called her fairly regularly this raised no suspicion on her part that anything might be amiss insofar as her grandmother was concerned. She asked how Martha was, and I told her she was just fine. But this, of course, made it plain that Martha had not gone to Los Angeles to visit Sue.

Sergeant Hunseker came by to see me the following morning about ten.

'We can't find this Mr. Grau,' he said. 'But we know he's a small man about sixty, with a heavy head of snow-white hair and a white handlebar mustache. He bought the car about a week ago from the old opera singer. Ferdinand Wilmot. Wilmot's hobby is collecting and refurbishing old automobiles. The old man gave Wilmot $10,000 for the car. In cash.'

As I have indicated, I have been involved with criminal oddities of every description for almost forty years and I'm not easily jarred or shocked. But I must say that Hunseker's announcement gave me a most uneasy feeling.

'In the meantime,' said Hunseker, 'we're having a rough time pinning down that wacky note. The lab boys have checked it out with every available piece of information they have on manufacturers of paper and all kinds of special fabrics, and they can't find anything like it. And they checked every typewriter in the Gibbs' house and every standard typewriter make, and can't find a machine on which this could have been written. Seems strange, doesn't it?'

I told him about Sue, and my call to her, and he agreed with me that neither his department nor the Los Angeles police should talk to Sue.

'There's no sense in alarming her,' Hunseker said. 'I'm sure Mrs. Gibbs will show up any minute.'

On Friday, five days after Martha disappeared, I was preparing to go to bed. It was one minute of eleven, and as is my habit, I went into my den and turned the television set on to the eleven o'clock news.

'What kind of a day has it been?' asked the newscaster. He went on to answer his own question. He covered a new international crisis, a local election, and then he said, 'And in Hollywood today, Charles Silk died. Silk, a private detective and sometime actor, had been seriously considered for the part of the fictional sleuth of the same name in the popular TV series, *The Adventures of Chuck Silk*. Silk crashed to his death in a fall from the terrace of his penthouse apartment on the Sunset Strip in the film capital sometime late this evening ...'

As is the irritating custom with shows of this kind there were no further details. I put in a call to Sergeant Hunseker and got him, finally, just as he arrived home.

'Yes,' he said, 'we got word about an hour ago. I'm trying to get an okay to go on out to the Coast to see if there's any connection between Silk's death and Mrs. Gibbs' disappearance. I'll let you know if I find out anything.'

As much as my professional career has taught me patience and inured me to what the average person considers unbearable suspense, I must say that the next two days dragged on interminably for me. Nothing of any consequence happened. Sergeant Hunseker got permission to go, and left for Los Angeles on Sunday morning.

Sunday night about ten P.M. I was up in my den idly passing the time with my stamp collection, when I happened to look out the window facing the Gibbs' house. I looked over toward the chimney, then back to the page of early Roman stamps again, then my head jerked up, and I stared at the chimney. Incredible as it seemed, on a hot mid-August evening, smoke was coming from the Gibbs' chimney.

With an excitement which would have been much more becoming in a younger man, I got up from my desk, and put a pair of trousers on over my pyjamas. I was halfway down the flight of stairs when the phone rang. This inexcusable excitement mounted in me at such a ridiculous rate that I became more than a little irritated with myself. I tripped and fell down the last three steps, hastening to the phone. Fortunately, I did not damage any of my ancient bones.

'Hello,' I said, irritably, to the mouthpiece of the telephone.

'Hello,' said Martha Hill Gibbs' deep voice. 'Hello, Frank? This is Martha ...'

She sounded extremely weary, wearier than I have ever heard her before.

'Martha, where are you?' I asked.

'Here, right here. Home,' she said.

'Home? You mean across the street? In your own house? Right now?'

'Yes, of course, Frank. I just got in a few minutes ago. I'm terribly, terribly tired but I must talk to you. Could you come over in about an hour? Just let me rest for an hour, and come over ...'

'Of course, Martha,' I said, 'I'll come right now.'

'No,' she said with what seemed to me a sudden desperate note in her voice. 'Please don't come now. Come in an hour.'

'All right, Martha,' I said, puzzled, 'but there's smoke coming from your chimney ...'

'I know, Frank, I'm burning some old boxes and papers Mrs. Klein left in the kitchen.'

'Oh, all right, I'll be over in an hour.'

It was about ten minutes of twelve (I just couldn't wait the full hour) that I burst into the Gibbs' house. Martha was lying on the sofa in the living room. At first I thought she might be asleep. But as I hesitated at the door, she rose slowly and sat up.

'Come in, Frank, please,' she said.

In the lamplight she looked more exhausted than I believe I have ever seen any human being look. But there was a brightness in her eyes that startled me. I know that this will sound inexcusably dramatic, but it was as though her whole being was burning with a fierce inner fire which showed only in her eyes. For the rest, her skin had a greyish pallor, and there were deep purple-black shadows beneath her eyes.

'Martha, Martha,' I said, 'where have you been? I ...'

She reached out her hand.

'Frank, it's so good to see you again. But please don't press me. Please sit down. Make yourself a drink, if you wish ... but please, hurry and sit down. I have had the most frightening, the most fascinating, the most exhilarating experience of my life. I must tell someone. I ... please, Frank, sit down.'

As I sat it occurred to me that the living room was filled with a strange odor. It passed through my mind fleetingly that the odor was similar to one I smelled often years ago, when a regular part of getting my hair cut was a singe, when the barber burned the edges of my freshly cut hair with the flame of a lighted taper. It was, quite plainly, I thought then, the smell of burning hair. I looked over toward the fireplace. The last embers of a small fire were dying there.

But Martha had my hand and was pulling me down beside her on the French provincial sofa.

'Frank,' she said, 'you must promise you'll never tell anyone this story as long as you live.'

'Well, Martha ...'

'Please, Frank, you must promise ...'

I nodded vaguely, and sat down beside her.

'I just attended a reunion of all my murderers,' she said.

'Oh, Martha, come on now, be sensible ...'

'You remember last Sunday morning when I waved to you as I was leaving?' she said. 'You know who that was? That man who picked me up?'

I looked into the wild flame of her eyes. I hesitated, then I said, 'You mean French? Johnny French?'

She seemed very pleased that I knew.

'Of course! Francis Xavier Malloy,' she said, 'as you have been all my life, you're a dear, wonderful, understanding and wise friend. I knew I could tell you this.'

I do not know now whether to attempt to tell this story as Martha told it to me, to report the dialogue verbatim, or whether to state the facts without color, emotion or dramatization of any kind, as I gathered them from Martha.

I have rested and flexed my arthritic fingers again now for a half hour while I have thought about this, and I believe a combination of Martha's own words and my honest narrative where it would make the picture clearest is desirable.

French took her to the airport, she said, and politely bade her goodbye at the gate whence her flight was scheduled to depart. In Los Angeles, as she entered the arrival gate, she was quite startled to see a sleek, black-haired young man with sharp green eyes, full lips and a generally dashing and insolent manner. It was Rory Williams, the murderer in her last book, *The Meek Shall Inherit Murder.* Johnny French had told her Williams would meet her in L.A., so she wasn't as surprised as she might otherwise have been.

Williams escorted her to a gleaming black new limousine, and when they were about a quarter mile away from the airport, he pulled the car over to the side of the road and pulled down heavy, black silk cloth blinds with which the car, strangely enough, was equipped.

'You're not to know where you're being taken,' he said to Martha, in the friendliest manner, as he got back in behind the wheel.

The ride took about an hour, as closely as Martha could estimate. They seemed, she thought, to be travelling long winding and ascending roads, and when Williams finally stopped, she saw they were parked before a lovely rambling house high on a mountain.

Wiliams took her into an exceptionally large, nicely furnished modern living room. Seated in groups around various lounges and chairs and standing in knots were approximately eighty people.

'It was, for all the world,' Martha went on with her story, 'just like any large cocktail party you might ever have attended. They were drinking and smoking and talking and laughing. But ... but it was the strangest thing. They were all dressed in the clothes of different periods. Some like people dressed in the twenties ... the way Johnny French was dressed. Some like the thirties. Some like the forties, and ...'

She paused as she recalled the meeting.

'... and there was something very, very familiar about

them, all of them. Before I realized what it was ... in spite of the note, and in spite of Johnny French and Rory Williams ... a little white haired man with a white mustache, Herman Grau – you remember him – he got up from a chair in a corner of the room. He clapped his hands sharply, and he said: "Ladies and gentlemen. Rise, please. Here is your creator!"'

I said, 'Martha, you look very tired. Wouldn't you like to go to bed, and tell me the rest of the story in the morning?'

She said, 'Frank, please don't interrupt me. I must tell this to someone. I told Ed, but that's different. I must tell someone here, in this world. I must tell you. Please ...'

I walked to Ed's bar in the corner of the living room and poured a water glass half full of whisky. I did not bother going after ice. I sat down on the sofa beside Martha again, and said, 'Of course, Martha, go on.'

Martha wrote seventy-nine detective novels between September of 1921 and last month. The first forty-eight of these featured Nurse Mary Brown as detective and the last thirty-one featured Charlie Silk. Each novel had one murderer. They were all there, at the reception, Martha said, except Johnny French, who had stayed back in New York. And Wilbur Hatch.

'You remember Wilbur?' Martha asked.

I did. He was the murderer in *Seven, Eight, Death Can't Wait*. He was a hypochondriac.

'Wilbur couldn't come,' Martha said. 'He wasn't feeling well.'

That evening, said Martha, after the cocktail party, they had the most wonderful dinner. Herman Grau acted as Master of Ceremonies, or Host or whatever you might call the spokesman of an assemblage of that kind. When they were on the dessert course, Grau got up and made a speech.

Martha repeated it for me, almost verbatim, but I really do not dare attempt to repeat it thus here. The gist is what is important.

Grau told Martha that the assembled group, the murderers she had created, had long smarted under the injustice of her treatment of them. Each of them had met death in one fashion or another, either via execution by the State, or by the hand of Silk or Nurse Brown, or some allied law enforcement officer. Each of them had died, officially or otherwise, simply because he or she had committed one or more simple murders.

It was Grau's firm belief, and indeed he maintained it was the well considered judgment of the entire group of murderers, that Charlie Silk and Nurse Mary Brown were guilty of many crimes far worse than murder, and that they (Martha's murderers) were therefore going to take it upon themselves to kill detectives Silk and Brown. They were going to take Martha along so that she could personally witness each of the two executions.

You will find it difficult to understand this, and perhaps it was the Scotch I consumed as Martha told the story, but by the time she told me about the murder of Charlie Silk, I almost believed it had happened, exactly as she described it to me. This very minute as I write about it, I am not at all sure that I do not believe it still. After all, I had heard the newscast myself. Charlie Silk was dead.

The charges against Charlie Silk, as Grau explained them, were:

(1) About ten years ago in Phoenix, Arizona, when he was twenty-six, he had married a young girl of sixteen, had quickly sired two children by her, and then deserted her. One of the children, a girl, had died of malnutrition at the age of six, about two years ago.

(2) Silk, who had since come to Hollywood, become a bit actor and opened a private detective agency, had managed to get a divorce, and had married a moderately wealthy woman of about fifty-five. He had squandered the woman's money through one bad investment after another, and then divorced her. She was presently in the alcoholic ward of the county hospital.

The charges against Nurse Mary Brown were even more unattractive. She'd been a nurse since 1920 when she was only eighteen years old. But, fatherless and motherless, and brought up in a foster home where the adults were cold if not outright cruel to her, she was about as amoral and feelingless as a person could be. Strangely enough, nursing gave her the opportunity to indulge her amoral tastes as few other occupations might.

For one thing she was able to filch narcotics from the

hospitals in which she worked. And since she used them only
to stimulate herself and whichever man she was consorting
with at any given time, she apparently never stole enough to
arouse suspicion.

She had, said Mr. Grau, caused the deaths of at least six
innocent persons either directly or indirectly, and it was high
time she was punished.

As Martha finished narrating Mr. Grau's comments
about Nurse Mary Brown, I looked over at the clock on the
mantle over the fireplace. It was 2:17 A.M. Martha had been
talking for more than two hours, and I had hardly
interrupted her at all.

I looked at her now and I ached with compassion for her.
Her cheeks were sunken, and the glow that had lain behind
her eyes had diminished, almost as though the fire which
caused it had died like the fire she had burned earlier in the
fireplace.

She was tired beyond human endurance, and I should
have refused to carry this meeting any further. Actually, I
tried to end it by showing her how far-fetched were her
ramblings.

I said, gently, 'Martha, your Nurse Mary Brown was never
like that. She was a sweet girl, something like you yourself
...'

Martha shook her head.

'No,' she said, 'I didn't write her like that because I didn't
know. But she *was* like that! She was! She was a wicked,
wicked woman!'

It occurred to me then in an alarming flash that I, too, now
was talking about a fictional character as though she were
real. I reached over and patted Martha's hand.

'Come on, Martha,' I said, 'you're tired. Let me take you
up to your room. After all, Mary Brown is just a name you
made up. There's no real Nurse Mary Brown.'

'Yes, there is,' said Martha. 'There are. There are
thousands of Mary Browns, and scores of them are nurses.
And this one, this evil one is dead. They killed her yesterday.
And she *was* my Mary Brown.'

She wanted to go on and tell me more but I prevailed upon
her to go to bed with the promise that I would come over first

thing in the morning to hear the rest of the story. I did not sleep at all that night.

Martha maintained that her murderers had planned the death of Charlie Silk, and Charlie Silk was dead. That was a coincidence. A strange one, but a coincidence nevertheless. As far as I knew there was no real Nurse Mary Brown. Or at least no Nurse Mary Brown who had been killed by Martha Hill Gibbs' murderers.

Yet the next day, just before noon when Martha urged me to come over again, I heard the rest of the story from her. Now it was not two o'clock in the morning. It was almost high noon of a bright August day in a quiet suburb, and yet Martha's story gave me the same eerie feeling its beginning had given me the night before.

Grau himself, she said, had taken her to Charlie Silk's penthouse apartment on the Sunset Strip. He had engaged Charlie in a conversation about the possiblity of taking over the part of the character bearing his own name in the TV film series. He had maneuvered Charlie to the low brick wall on the edge of the penthouse terrace, and with one firm push had hurled him over. Martha said she sat there and watched the entire event.

Then, she said, one of the murderers, a Captain Samuel Hotchkiss, had flown with her from Los Angeles to Boston, direct flight.

'Do you remember Captain Hotchkiss, Frank?' she asked me.

I did, and quite well. He was a craggy-faced, red-haired, red-bearded ex-New England seaman, about sixty-five years old, who had been around the world a dozen times. He had murdered a wealthy owner of a line of pleasure steamships in a novel of Martha's called *Death Sails at Dawn*.

'When we got off the plane in Boston,' said Martha, 'Captain Hotchkiss took me directly to this brownstone house in Boston where Nurse Mary Brown lived. He told her he was an old friend of her dead husband's, and that I was his sister. She made tea for us. While she was out of the room, he put some kind of a drug in her cup of tea. She fell asleep, and when she was sleeping, he took a large hypodermic needle out of a little bag he was carrying, and plunged it into a vein on the inside of her left arm. He said it was a shot of heroin, sufficient to kill a dozen people. He then wiped the hypo and placed it in her right hand so it would look like she killed herself.'

Now with the bright sunlight shining through the windows and making boxes on the living room rug as we talked, Martha's story simply seemed like the wanderings of a mind which had torn loose from its moorings and was drifting harmlessly. A good mind, trained through an adult lifetime of very successful detective story writing, to concoct all kinds of fanciful plots.

'That's very interesting, Martha,' I said, 'but you look very tired. Don't you think I should call Dr. Goldstein? Just to give you a routine check-up?'

'Don't you dare, Frank,' she said. 'I'm fine. I am tired, but I'm fine.' She smiled then.

'You don't believe any of what I've told you, do you?' she said. 'You think I'm a crazy old woman who's having hallucinations.'

I patted her hand.

'I don't think anything of the kind, Martha. I think you're just tired. Is it okay if I call Dr. Goldstein?'

She smiled again.

'Sure, Francis Xavier Malloy. You always were a dear. A dull dear with no imagination whatsoever, but a dear anyway. Call the doctor.'

Dr. Goldstein came that afternoon. Martha's heartbeat was extremely weak and irregular. He gave her an injection and prescribed complete rest.

'I'm worried about her, Frank,' he told me. 'I don't know what she's been through since Ed died, but she's in very serious trouble.'

It was so serious Martha died a week later, exactly the same way Ed had died. Quietly, in her bed, sometime during the night. She, too, had a smile on her face. A very pleased smile, it seemed to me, strangely enough.

Our police department, in the meantime, had checked out the death of Charles Silk with the Los Angeles police. Although the L.A. officers felt that either Silk's first wife or someone close to her, or his second wife, the elderly woman who was in the county hospital alcoholic ward, or someone close to her might have had a strong enough motive to kill Silk, they had no evidence to indicate that he had not either fallen or jumped from his penthouse terrace.

They had talked to everyone who had seen him the day of his death, as far as they knew, except for an elderly gentleman with snow white hair and a snow white handlebar mustache. This gentleman had inquired at the desk if Silk was in his apartment, but he seemed to have vanished from the face of the earth. Hunseker thought it strange that this description should be familiar to the owner of the ebony limousine, but simply could not find any such person.

Naturally I did not ignore Martha's story of the murder of Nurse Mary Brown. The same day she told it to me I went into town, to the public library, and looked through every page of every newspaper for Tuesday, Wednesday and Thursday. I scanned each page carefully, looking for a report on the death by heroin of Mary Brown. I found nothing.

I went over to the out-of-town newsstands and purchased all the Boston papers for those days. In the Boston papers there were two homicides reported. A man had gone berserk and killed his wife and four children, and a teen-age hoodlum had stabbed a policeman in a hallway. But nothing on Mary Brown, or a death by hypodermic needle.

Still Martha's story, the story itself and the fierce conviction with which she told it continued to haunt me.

Martha had left a considerable estate, over and above what Ed had already left. I had been designated the Executor of the estate. It came to well over a half million dollars. One hundred thousand dollars of it went toward the establishment of a continuing scholarship at the same college where Martha had majored in English Literature, and where Sue was now going. The rest went to Sue, under my guardianship and with me acting as trustee of the estate.

All of Martha's papers, manuscripts and notes she bequeathed to me. I was worried about Sue as I anticipated her arrival for the funeral. She had had to withstand the shock of the deaths of three people whom presumably she loved, in a pathetically short time. Her granddad, her grandmother, and Charles Silk. Under the circumstances I was much relieved rather than shocked by our conversation on the way back from the cemetery.

'Uncle Frank,' she said quietly, 'do you remember how Grandma objected to my marrying Charlie Silk? How intense she was, even though she seemed a little incoherent about it?'

'Yes, I certainly do. I most certainly do.'

'Well, she was right, Uncle Frank. He was a terrible man. When they were investigating his death, a very nice young man – his name is Rog Shane – he was one of the detectives on the case – he became very irritated with me because I was crying and carrying on about Charlie's death. He forced me to come with him to the county hospital to have a talk with Charlie's second wife ... that poor, poor woman. And he told me about the girl in Arizona ...'

'I know,' I said, 'your grandmother was a wise and unusual woman.'

She wanted to finish summer school, so she returned to California the day after the funeral. I proceeded with all the legal arrangements in connection with the will. A couple of weeks later, I sat in Martha's study in the Gibbs' house going through her papers. She was the type of woman who apparently kept many of her letters. She kept them in composition file boxes, one box for each year.

I went back to the first ones in the 1922 box. That was the year my wife, Ann, and I had first met Ed and Martha Hill Gibbs. Reading the letters was like reliving a whole, extraordinarily interesting and happy lifetime. There were clear reflections of my own early years with Ann and our two children; of Martha's pre-marital romance with Ed, and his youthful struggles as a doctor. There were all manner of letters, birthday, anniversary and other cards marking milestones in our lives. The birth of Martha's daughter, Ann, in 1923, one year after Martha and Ed were married. And Ann's own marriage at the age of eighteen, the same age her daughter Sue now was, to a nice young man of twenty, named Jimmy Hart. That was in 1941, and even though Jimmy went into the Navy almost immediately, Sue was born early in 1942.

Jimmy had been wounded in France, and shipped back to a Naval Hospital in Boston early in 1945. The German war, you'll recall, ended in May of that year. Jimmy was in the hospital there till the middle of June. They were tender and touching, these events of the war years, as reflected in Ann's letters to Martha and to Jimmy and his to Ann. And then I came, quite without warning of any kind, upon a letter which jolted my heart in my chest. I felt like I had been hit by a hard fist.

The letter was dated July 19, 1945. It was to Martha, who was then living in this very house, from her daughter, Ann, who was still living in Boston. It said:

'Dearest Mom –

'I have not wanted to write you about this, but if I don't I will go out of my mind. I am losing Jimmy and I don't know any way to stop from losing him. You remember how much pain from his back he suffered all the while he was in the hospital. They started to give him drugs to ease the pain, and it did. I think they gave him the drugs right up until the time he was discharged. But I don't think that would have been bad, but one of his nurses, a girl, began to pay a lot of special attention to him and make a big fuss over him. It is the oddest thing, but this girl's name is Mary Brown, the same as the nurse in your stories. One time he even told me that this Mary Brown gets him extra drugs. She even gave him a shot of morphine one night right after the doctor told us he was going to have to start easing off drugs.

'She is a very beautiful girl, Mom, but she is a very bad girl. Since Jimmy came home from the hospital, she has been seeing him and going out with him. I suspected it for weeks, but just tonight, about an hour ago, Jimmy and I had a big fight and he admitted it. He says she gives him everything he needs and I don't and never could. I'm pretty sure she still gives him narcotics. I think she even uses them herself, but maybe just marijuana, but anyway he told me they have these wild parties, just the two of them. I love Jimmy, Mom, and I don't know what I will do if he leaves me. I don't know what Susie will do either because she loves him and needs him even more than I do. Please help me, Mom. Any way you possibly can.

Love,
Ann'

It came back to me then. I remembered Martha saying she was going to Boston to visit the kids. She didn't tell me anything about Mary Brown. She evidently didn't tell anyone, even Ed.

The night she got there Jimmy and Martha's daughter, Ann, were killed in an automobile accident. He ran off the road at high speed and crashed into a large oak tree. Martha brought Susie back to live with her and Ed. Susie was four years old.

And Martha's last Nurse Mary Brown detective novel was published in January of 1946.

I went to the bookcase and found it. It was *Death Sails at Dawn*. The murderer was a red-bearded, ex-sea captain from New England named Samuel Hotchkiss, and the dedication in the book read,

> 'To Susan
> and her future
> which I vow to protect'

There was nothing more about Mary Brown in any letters or notes beyond Ann's last letter to her mother. Now I was even more tormented by Martha's story. I went to Boston the following morning. It took me exactly eight days, and if it were not for the fact that I found a number of colleagues in high ranks in the Boston police department with whom I had worked over the years, I would not have been able to secure the information I needed in that time, if at all.

I learned that Nurse Mary Brown had been discharged from the Naval Hospital in 1948 because she was arrested and convicted on a charge of possession of narcotics. In 1955, when she was about thirty, she had married a doctor named Wilkerson, who was about seventy years old at the time. He died a year later, apparently from natural causes. She bought a small house in Newton, and it was there she was found dead the day Martha said she had been killed.

The police decided she had died from a self-administered overdose of heroin. A number of tradesmen had come and gone into the house that day, and one man with a red beard had entered and left, but there was nothing particularly suspicious about him, and in any event a fairly aggressive search did not produce him. It did not make the papers because other more spectacular news crowded it out.

I also learned that an autopsy on Jimmy Hart, following his death in the automobile accident, revealed that he had been under the influence of narcotics, although it was morphine, not heroin.

On the plane returning from Boston, I turned these facts over and over in my mind. Since then, in virtually every waking moment, and they have been many for I cannot sleep, I have reviewed the case. Again and again and again!

Certainly Martha had the motive to kill both Charlie Silk and Nurse Mary Brown. By killing Silk she had prevented Sue from entering into what almost surely would have been a tragic marriage. By killing Mary Brown Wilkerson she avenged the death of Ann and Jimmy Hart.

But, I ask myself, why would she have waited sixteen years to kill Mrs. Wilkerson? And the answer, of course, is that she probably never would have killed Mary Brown Wilkerson except that the death of Ed unbalanced her. Or perhaps it was the combination of Ed's death, and Sue's sudden announcement that she was planning to marry Charles Silk.

How could I account for the fact that Martha herself was not seen at either the Silk murder locale or the Wilkerson murder scene, but that a man fitting the description of Martha's murderer, Herman Grau, was seen at the first; and her murderer, Samuel Hotchkiss, at the second?

In reviewing this phase of the case in my mind, I recalled Martha's appearance at a Famous Persons masquerade party, which our mutual neighbor, Mrs. Dorsch, gave at the Country Club two summers ago. Martha came dressed as Josef Stalin, and with a wig of coal black hair and a black handle-bar mustache, plus a little stuffing, she made a very convincing Stalin. There was no reason in the world why she could not have made up as convincingly as Grau and Hotchkiss. And her normally deep husky voice would have abetted those impersonations just as it did her Stalin impersonation.

As I pondered the possibility of the masquerade I recalled that hot August night not so long ago when I had seen the smoke coming out of the Gibbs chimney, and Martha had asked me not to come over for another hour, and the lingering smell of burning hair when I finally did enter her living room. She could have been burning the Grau and Hotchkiss moustahces and hairpieces on that occasion.

But I, myself, had seen Johnny French, or at least a man who resembled Johnny French, pick Martha up in front of her house. He was certainly real. But then he may easily have been a man resembling the Johnny French of Martha's story, whom Martha had hired to pick her up that morning, just to make me feel that her subsequent tale of fictional murderers was true. I am a creature of habit, and she knew I would be out at that hour of the morning.

But why would she go to such pains to set me up for acceptance of such a wild and improbable series of circumstances? Why, indeed! Why would the idea of having her fictional murderers avenge their capture, and own deaths, by murdering the living counterparts of the fictional detectives who exposed them occur to Martha in the first place? If indeed it did! Who, after all, knows what the human mind will do under certain stresses after more than six decades?

I checked and rechecked every element of the situation. I even went up to New Rochelle to talk to Ferdinand Wilmot, the retired opera singer from whom Herman Grau had bought the ancient limousine for $10,000 in cash. His description fitted Grau perfectly.

In the position of the Executor of Martha's estate it was not at all difficult for me to trace through every known bank account she possessed to find a $10,000 cash withdrawal arounnd the time the car was purchased from Mr. Wilmot. I found no such withdrawal, but then Martha could easily have had that amount in an account I knew nothing about, or for that matter she could even have had it saved and put away somewhere in cash. And if she was unbalanced enough to have decided to perpetrate the entire mad scheme in the first place, she certainly would not have hesitated to waste $10,000 carrying it out.

There were and there are still times when I fit all the pieces into place, and as a veteran, coldly logical, altogether mature ex-law enforcement officer, I say to myself: My friend, Martha Hill Gibbs became mentally deranged when her husband of almost forty years died, and she killed a man named Charles Silk and a woman named Mary Brown Wilkerson.

There are other times when I say: No! Life is full of coincidences much stranger than any of these. This is simply a case of an unsavory and unwholesome man named Charles Silk who fell from the penthouse terrace of his apartment, or possibly could not tolerate himself as a human being any longer and therefore decided to destroy himself. And a woman who led a wicked and dissolute life did likewise.

And then there are those increasingly frequent times when I say: As completely incredible as it seems, a group of fictional murderers came to life and executed the living counterparts of the fictional detectives who exposed and disposed of them in a series of very successful novels.

Then again I say: No, it is utterly ridiculous! There are no supernatural forces in this world. My friend, Martha Hill Gibbs, killed those two people.

I had come to that conclusion for the thousandth time yesterday, when Sergeant Hunseker dropped by. From the viewpoint of the Missing Persons Bureau, and for that matter, of the Police Department as a whole, the Martha Hill Gibbs case was of no official interest whatsoever. As far as they were concerned, Martha had just gone away on a trip which was entirely her business, and returned voluntarily. And a man in Hollywood had either accidentally fallen, or deliberately hurled himself from his penthouse terrace. And a woman in Newton had, again either deliberately or accidentally, give himself an overdose of heroin.

We walked about all sorts of things, Sergeant Hunseker and I, and at one point, we touched on the Martha Hill Gibbs case.

'You know, Commissioner,' he said, 'one thing about that case. You remember that crazy invitation signed, "Affectionately, your murderers," we found?'

'Yes, of course,' I said.

'Well, I was talking to Phil Collins, a friend of mine in the Lab the other day. They've checked that note out with the FBI, Scotland Yard, the French Sureté Nationale and Interpol, and you know what, Commissioner? As far as any of them have been able to determine, no typewriter ever built by man could have written that note, and it was not handwritten, printed or duplicated in any other way known to science. Isn't that weird?'

'It is, Sergeant,' I said. 'Yes, indeed, it is.'

And last night I fell asleep in my chair – at least I think I fell asleep – while watching the eleven o'clock news, and I had the strangest dream. I dreamed that Martha Hill Gibbs came into the room and sat down in that blue chair right across the room, and greeted me most warmly.

And she said:

'I just had to come by to tell you, Frank. I'm so happy. Sue is marrying a young man just like you. He's just been promoted to Detective Second Grade in the Los Angeles Police Department. She met him while they were investigating the death of Charlie Silk.

I woke with a start – or at least I thought I did. And I thought I saw Martha walking out the door, but through it, unopened. And it wasn't more than a half hour later when my phone rang:

'Mr. Malloy, please,' said a woman's voice.

'Yes, yes, this is Mr. Malloy.'

'This is long distance. Will you accept a collect call from a Miss Susan Gibbs in Malibu, California?'

I tried to say 'yes,' but no sound came from my dry throat until my third attempt. Then Sue came on.

'Uncle Frank,' she said, 'I'm calling you collect because I'm in a phone booth on the Pacific Coast Highway, and neither Rog nor I had enough money on us to pay for the call. We were driving along, and he just asked me to marry him, and I made him stop the car at the first phone booth we came to –'

I don't know. I don't know.

B.M. GILL

THE TWELFTH JUROR

Winner of the 1985 Crime Writers' Association GOLD
DAGGER AWARD for the best crime novel.

On trial is Edward Carne, accused of murdering his wife.
On the jury are eleven dedicated and unbiased men and
women, and a twelfth, Robert Quinn, who should not be
there at all.

The evidence put before the jury is tantalizingly
inconclusive, and the accused is conspicuously absent
from the witness box. All this is confusing enough, but
what of Robert Quinn's obsessive involvement in the
trial, an obsession he will not – and indeed cannot –
reveal?

'Gripping, with a chilling climax. Gill's feel for the
offbeat sinister is superb' THE TIMES

A Royal Mail service in association with the Book Marketing Council & The Booksellers Association.
Post-A-Book is a Post Office trademark.

PETER HAINING Ed.

THE GHOST STORIES OF CHARLES DICKENS
BOOKS 1 & 2

In these two volumes of chilling ghost stories, Charles
Dickens again reveals his lifelong fascination with the
macabre and the supernatural – a fascination which
originated at his nursemaid's knee. The stories that they
were to haunt him for the rest of his life and profoundly
influence his writing.

These two collections, which include some famous
stories as THE SIGNAL-MAN and THE GHOST
CHAMBER, represent an attempt by Dickens to exorcise
the spell of the supernatural; and show the reader a
little-known and compelling side of one of the greatest
and best-loved of British writers.

CORONET BOOKS

ALFRED HITCHCOCK

STORIES TO BE READ WITH THE DOOR LOCKED
BOOKS 1 & 2

A WARNING FROM ALFRED HITCHCOCK

'I am in the business of entertainment, and in all the long years of relentlessly searching for likely material, one's appetite is apt to become jaded. So the discovery of original stories, stories that will chill OR PERHAPS EVEN KILL, provides a rare gratification.'

'Now the word "KILL" may of course be an exaggeration. On the other hand, excitement makes the heart beat faster. AN ACCELERATED HEARTBEAT COULD CONCEIVABLY PUMP AN EXISTING EMBOLISM INTO SOME CRITICAL ARTERY.'

'CAUTION THEN IS THE WATCHWORD...'

These are stories of nail-biting suspense from such expert craftsmen as ROALD DAHL, ISAAC ASIMOV, MICHAEL GILBERT and HAROLD Q. MASUR. Stories to haunt you deep into the night. STORIES TO BE READ WITH THE DOOR LOCKED!

CORONET BOOKS

ALSO AVAILABLE FROM CORONET BOOKS